Golf
STEPS TO SUCCESS

Paul G. Schempp
University of Georgia

Peter Mattsson
Swedish Golf Federation

Human Kinetics

Library of Congress Cataloging-in-Publication Data

Schempp, Paul G.
　　Golf : steps to success / Paul Schempp, Peter Mattsson.
　　　　p. cm.
　　ISBN 0-7360-5902-4 (soft cover)
　　1. Golf. I. Mattsson, Peter, 1970- II. Title.
　　GV965.S273 2005
　　796.352--dc22

2005001615

ISBN-10: 0-7360-5902-4
ISBN-13: 978-0-7360-5902-2

Acquisitions Editor: Jana Hunter
Developmental Editor: Cynthia McEntire
Assistant Editor: Scott Hawkins
Copyeditor: Alisha Jeddeloh
Proofreader: Joanna Hatzopoulos Portman
Graphic Designer: Nancy Rasmus
Graphic Artist: Kim McFarland
Cover Designer: Keith Blomberg
Photographer (cover): © Stuart Franklin/Getty Images
Art Manager: Kareema McLendon
Course Diagrams: Argosy
Line Art: Roberto Sabas
Printer: Versa Press

Human Kinetics books are available at special discounts for bulk purchase. Special editions or book excerpts can also be created to specification. For details, contact the Special Sales Manager at Human Kinetics.

Printed in the United States of America

10 9 8 7 6 5 4 3

Human Kinetics
Web site: www.HumanKinetics.com

United States: Human Kinetics
P.O. Box 5076
Champaign, IL 61825-5076
800-747-4457
e-mail: humank@hkusa.com

Canada: Human Kinetics
475 Devonshire Road, Unit 100
Windsor, ON N8Y 2L5
800-465-7301 (in Canada only)
e-mail: info@hkcanada.com

Europe: Human Kinetics
107 Bradford Road
Stanningley
Leeds LS28 6AT, United Kingdom
+44 (0)113 255 5665
e-mail: hk@hkeurope.com

Australia: Human Kinetics
57A Price Avenue
Lower Mitcham, South Australia 5062
08 8372 0999
e-mail: info@hkaustralia.com

New Zealand: Human Kinetics
Division of Sports Distributors NZ Ltd.
P.O. Box 300 226 Albany
North Shore City, Auckland
0064 9 448 1207
e-mail: info@humankinetics.co.nz

For Dr. DeDe Owens (1946-1999),
one of golf's most dedicated,
talented, and knowledgeable teachers.
She remains an inspiration to
instructors and players everywhere.

 # Contents

Climbing the Steps to Golf Success

For beginning and intermediate players as well as teachers and coaches, *Golf: Steps to Success* will help ensure a solid foundation of fundamentals and add skills and knowledge to what a player has already achieved. The steps to success are arranged in order, beginning with putting the ball into the hole and progressing back to a smooth and accurate tee shot.

At each step, beginners will benefit from clear, concise information on the basics for every part of the game—skills, strategies, and rules. The explanations and accompanying illustrations not only provide comprehensive instruction for executing each skill, but they also reveal how these skills can be used strategically to speed success on the course.

Golf: Steps to Success offers thorough explanations of fundamental and specialty shots, so intermediate players will have the opportunity to refine their skills with game-specific drills as they move toward advanced performance. They will gain insight into when, why, and how to hit the right shot. They will learn to analyze a golf course and assemble their skills into a game plan that will minimize errors and maximize playing potential.

For teachers, *Golf: Steps to Success* provides an all-inclusive instructional package. The information, drills, activities, and grading methods can be easily adapted to existing instructional programs. Teachers will also find useful information on the history of golf, the latest equipment, rules, course management strategies, sport psychology, and Web-based golf resources. Add to that information key cues in executing a full range of golf shots, as well as strategy, self-paced drills, and methods of evaluating each student, and you have an invaluable teaching resource.

As coaches to amateur and professional golfers, we know that a coach is in constant search of new solutions to familiar problems and tested methods for improving player performance. *Golf: Steps to Success* represents a compilation of the knowledge, skills, strategies, and drills we have used in working with successful golfers at all levels of the game, from complete beginners to accomplished professionals. In each step, coaches will find at least one nugget of knowledge, fresh idea, or unique drill that will help them help their players improve.

Whether you are a recreational golfer or play at a competitive level, you will improve your performance and enjoy the game more as you develop greater competency in the skills and strategies required for successful play. *Golf: Steps to Success* provides a progressive plan for developing golf skills and gaining more confidence on the course. For each step, follow this sequence:

1. Read the explanation of the skill covered in the step, why the step is important, and how to execute the step.

2. Study the illustrations, which show how to execute each skill.

3. Read the instructions for each drill. Practice the drills and record your scores.

4. Have a qualified observer—a teacher, coach, or trained partner—evaluate your skill technique once you've completed each set of drills. The observer can use the success checks included with each drill to evaluate your execution of the skill.

5. At the end of the step, review your performance and total your scores from the drills. Once you've achieved the indicated level of success, move on to the next step.

Legendary golfer Ben Hogan once said, "There are no born golfers. Some have more natural ability than others, but they've all been made." As Mr. Hogan won 62 professional tournaments, including all four major championships, his words carry considerable weight. Use *Golf: Steps to Success* to make you a better golfer. The steps can help you learn the game, expand your skills, teach the game with key cues and effective evaluations, or coach with proven player-development strategies. Even advanced players will find drills to hone their shot-making skills and tactics to give them a competitive edge.

People play golf for many reasons. For some, golf is an enjoyable, healthy physical activity in a beautiful outdoor setting. For others, golf provides a venue for social interaction with companions. Others find golf a platform for conducting business in a relaxed atmosphere. And for those who are keen for competition, there is no shortage of tournaments. Wherever your golfing aspirations lead you, *Golf: Steps to Success* will bring you closer to becoming the player you desire to be.

◰ Acknowledgments

Although we are listed as the authors, this book contains ideas, activities, and effort from a great many people. It is both fitting and appropriate that we acknowledge the many people who have helped us in this endeavor.

First and foremost, we would like to recognize the players with whom we have had the privilege of working over many years. In our efforts to help them find success in golf, they have helped us to become better teachers and coaches. There are many players to whom we owe a debt of thanks, but in particular Niclas Fasth, Mathias Gronberg, Richard S. Johnson, Per-Ulrik Johansson, Fredrik Jacobson, Catrin Nilsmark, Jesper Parnevik, Carl Pettersson, and Annika Sörenstam, plus a number of not-yet-so-known players on the Swedish golf team for helping us understand the steps to success in golf. The skills, points, and drills included in this book have all been field tested by these talented players.

Several coaches have been instrumental in focusing our ideas on how success in golf is achieved. Pia Nilsson first brought us together and has remained a friend and valued colleague. The group of coaches working with the Swedish golf team is a constant source of inspiration and new ideas. Also the Swedish Golf Federation deserves a fair bit of recognition for its great ambition to support players and coaches and to develop the game of golf.

To the staff at Human Kinetics, particularly our editor Cynthia McEntire, we are deeply indebted. This book was written on trains, planes, and in many coffee shops near golf tournaments on three continents. Coaching players and writing books are separate challenges, and the HK staff was patient and understanding as we struggled to balance both.

The final acknowledgment is expressed with the deepest sense of love and gratitude to Peter's family. Maria, Filip, and Elina have sacrificed precious time with a husband and father so that Peter could pursue excellence in his profession and he and Paul could complete this book. Their gifts of time, love, and support have always been appreciated and are here recognized.

☐ The Sport of Golf

Every round of golf begins with a bit of nervous anticipation. There is excitement in the promise of playing well, accompanied by jitters from not knowing what will actually happen out on the course. Walking onto the first tee box, pushing a tee into the ground, perching a ball upon it, stepping back for a final stretch, taking a long look down the fairway to sight your target, stepping to the ball—you are ready to play and see where the round takes you.

Golf has been a popular pastime for centuries. It was so popular in 1457 that King James II of Scotland banned it because it was interfering with archery practice and other military training. However, golf has won out over archery at St. Andrews, home of the first golf course in the world. In that sleepy little university town along the east coast of Scotland, you can find a game on one of the five public golf courses. The locals still stroll with dogs or baby carriages across the fairways of the famed Old Course on their way to the beach just past the first tee. Regardless of where you play—and today you can find golf courses just about anywhere in the world—you will find certain elements common to most courses.

GOLF COURSE

Carrying on a tradition begun at St. Andrews, today's regulation golf course has 18 holes. Each hole has a teeing ground and a closely mowed area called the green, into which a hole is cut and a flag is placed.

Along the course are par 3, par 4, and par 5 holes (figure 1). Par is the number of strokes that the golf course designer estimates a very good golfer will take to complete a particular hole. Say a course designer estimates that a very good golfer will take two strokes to get the ball in the hole once the ball is on the green. If the designer believes a very good player should take one stroke to get the ball on the green, the hole is a par 3. Put another way, on a par-3 hole a golfer should take one stroke to get the ball on the green and two strokes to get the ball in the hole. Designers also include holes that require

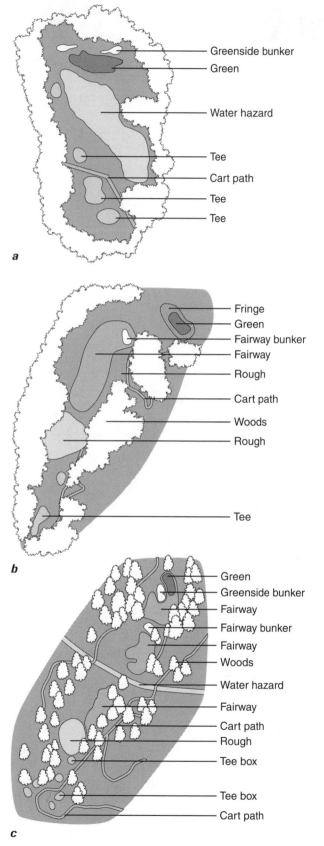

Figure 1 Sample golf holes: *(a)* par 3; *(b)* par 4; *(c)* par 5.

two or three strokes to reach the green (par 4 and par 5). In these cases, a fairway is cut between the teeing ground and the green so that a player can land the ball off the tee and then hit an approach from the fairway to the green.

The total length of a golf course varies from 5,000 yards to over 7,000 yards (4,572 to 6,400 meters). Short holes range from 80 to 240 yards (73 to 220 meters), medium holes stretch from 240 to 460 yards (220 to 420 meters), and long holes can run over 600 yards (550 meters). To provide various levels of challenge, multiple tee boxes are placed on each hole. For example, in Pinehurst, North Carolina, from the forward tees course 2 covers 5,035 yards (4,604 meters), but played from the back tees the same course is 7,189 yards (6,574 meters), a difference of over 2,000 yards (1800 meters)! Golf courses are designed in this manner so that players of all abilities can enjoy the same golf course. This is one factor that makes golf so popular.

Before venturing out to play a round of golf, you will need to acquire certain equipment, understand how a game is scored, and learn basic rules and etiquette. These elements are covered in this introduction and referred to throughout the book. You will also need to develop critical skills and strategies, which you will learn in the subsequent steps.

EQUIPMENT

To the new player and even to veteran players, equipment can be confusing and overwhelming due to the amount and variety available. However, a player needs only two things: clubs and a ball. A bag to carry your clubs, shoes to ensure good footing, and a few accessories can also increase your enjoyment and skill.

Clubs

The rules of golf state that you can carry no more than 14 clubs during a round of golf. Precisely which clubs are the right ones for you are a matter of your skill and the golf course you are playing. Fortunately, there are some standards to guide you when selecting clubs. There are four types of clubs: metals, irons, wedges, and putters (figure 2). Regardless of the type

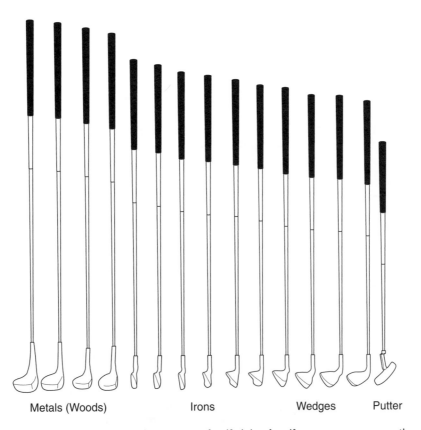

Metals (Woods)   Irons   Wedges   Putter

Figure 2 Metals, irons, wedges, and putters make up a set of golf clubs. A golfer can carry no more than 14 clubs on the course.

of club, clubs have three parts: grip, shaft, and head (figure 3).

Metal clubs have the largest heads and longest shafts of all the clubs. These clubs were once called woods because the clubhead was made of persimmon wood. Today these clubs are made with a variety of metals, although titanium is preferred due to its strength and elasticity.

Metal clubs are numbered 1, 3, 4, 5, 7, and 9, with the higher-numbered clubs having the higher loft. Loft is the angle between the clubface and a line at a 90-degree angle from the surface. The more the clubface is angled to the sky when it is resting on the ground, the more loft it has. A club with more loft will send the ball higher but a shorter distance than a club with less loft. Club 1 is the driver and seldom has the number on the bottom, or sole, of the clubhead. Clubs 3, 4, 5, 7, and 9 are referred to as fairway metals and are used most often on the fairway.

The most common configuration of metal clubs in the average golfer's bag is driver, 3-metal, and 5-metal. Because they send the ball

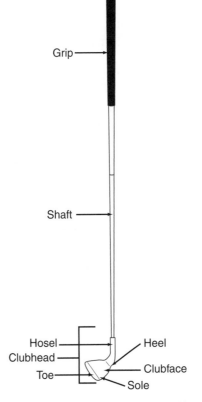

Grip

Shaft

Hosel   Heel
Clubhead   Clubface
Toe   Sole

Figure 3 All clubs have a grip, shaft, and head.

higher and are easier to hit, many players prefer to add the 7- or 9-metal to their bag and take out some of the long irons.

Iron clubs are numbered 1 through 9. The 1-iron has the least loft and the longest shaft while the 9-iron has the shortest shaft and the most loft; the 9-iron thus sends the ball the highest but also the shortest distance of all the irons. Due to their long shaft and low loft, the 1- and 2-irons are seldom recommended for the average player, and most irons are sold in sets numbered 3 through 9. Iron clubs get their name from the original metal—iron—used in making the head. However, today's iron clubheads are a composite of metals.

Two types of clubheads are used in irons: forged and perimeter-weighted. Forged irons place more weight in the center of the club-head while perimeter-weighted irons distribute the weight on the outside of the clubhead. For advanced players who consistently strike the ball in the middle of the clubhead, forged irons give a better feel and performance. For the average player who does not always hit the center of the clubhead, the perimeter-weighted clubhead is more forgiving and gives a better result with shots that are struck slightly off-center. In recent years, perimeter-weighted clubs have become the iron of choice for most players, including touring professionals.

Wedges are irons that have slightly modified soles to help move the clubhead through sand or green-side rough. Typical wedges include the approach wedge, pitching wedge, sand wedge, and lob wedge. Ladies Professional Golf Association (LPGA) tour player Annika Sörenstam carries four wedges in her golf bag, but most players carry only a pitching wedge and a sand wedge.

Because wedges have the greatest loft, they produce the most spin on the golf ball, allowing the ball to bite or stop on a hard green. Wedges also have the shortest shafts, which makes them easier to control. With the greatest loft and short-est shafts, they are designed for short or scoring shots. Practicing with the wedges is a sure way to lower your scores.

Putters come in all shapes and lengths. Play-ers can choose from a long putter, belly putter, or standard putter. With a long putter, the end

of the shaft is against the chest as the top hand and the lower hand grip the middle of the shaft. With a belly putter, the end of the shaft is pressed against the stomach. With a standard putter, the end of the shaft is gripped with both hands. The most common length by far is the standard putter. As for putter heads, many varieties are on the market, with new ones appearing each year. When selecting a putter, it is best to simply try several until you find one that feels comfort-able and puts the ball in the hole. Performance is more important than looks, so go for the putter that does the job for you.

A final thought on clubs: Get fitted. Most club shops can fit you for a set based on your swing. If you are buying new clubs, this service is usually free. If the shop does not offer this service, see a professional who is certified by the PGA (Pro-fessional Golf Association of America) or LPGA to fit clubs to players. You will be fitted for the proper length and flex of the shaft, optimal lie and loft for each clubhead, and grip size. The time and money you put into this process will pay off in years of good service from your clubs. The investment is well worth it.

Golf Balls

Over the years there have been major advances in golf ball technology. All advances have ben-efited the player. Today's golf balls fly farther and with less sidespin. (Sidespin is the force that redirects an otherwise perfectly good shot with a big, sweeping curve called a slice.) Like clubs, golf balls come in many varieties. The differences in golf balls are both internal and external. The design characteristics of a golf ball are on the packaging, not the ball itself, so read labels carefully.

Internally, golf balls have a one-, two-, or three-piece core. Multicore centers produce more backspin, which gives better players more control over their shots. Some multicore balls gain greater distance from the accelerated clubhead speed of a good golfer. Solid or single-piece core balls spin less but tend to fly a bit farther, characteristics appreciated by beginning and intermediate golfers and golfers with lower swing speeds.

Externally, golf ball covers come in soft and hard varieties. Soft covers provide a better feel, particularly on short shots and putting, but only good players can detect this characteristic. Soft covers tend to be more expensive and less durable. Hard covers are more durable, spin less, and are less expensive. These qualities appeal to the beginning to intermediate player.

Which ball should you use? With so many choices available, this can be a difficult question to answer. If you are just beginning, look for a solid-center golf ball with a durable cover. These balls are less expensive, last longer, go farther, and spin less, giving you straighter shots. At this level, your golf shots will be more affected by your swing technique than the ball, so focus more on your skills and don't fret too much about the ball. As your skill increases, try a variety of mid- to upper-priced balls until you find one that fits your game. If you get serious about your game, you can seek advice directly from ball manufacturers. This information is easily accessible on the Web. Two sources for popular golf balls are Titleist (www.titleist.com) and Top Flite (www.topflite.com).

Accessories

If you have a set of clubs and a golf ball, you have all the tools you need to play. However, you may want to consider a few accessories to make your game more efficient and comfortable.

Unless you want to walk a golf course with 14 different clubs hanging loose under your arm, you will need a golf bag. Two common types of golf bags are stand bags and cart bags. Stand bags are used by players who prefer to walk the course as they play a round of golf. These bags are smaller and lighter than cart bags and come equipped with a stand mechanism that opens automatically when the bottom of the bag is placed on the ground. The stand keeps the bag upright and angles the clubs toward the golfer for easy selection. A cart bag is larger and heavier and is designed to be strapped to the back of a golf cart for those who prefer to ride the course. All golf bags come with pockets for storing golf balls, tees, a sweater or rain suit, and other accessories. Loops for holding an umbrella and golf towel come on most golf bags, as does a hood cover.

Balance is a critical factor in a golf swing, and golf shoes are specifically designed to hold your feet firmly to the ground during the swing. Golf shoes have the added benefit of being waterproof, as rain or heavy dew can soak your feet in a hurry. Considering that an average round of golf takes four to five hours, the support offered by comfortable, well-fitted golf shoes makes them a recommended accessory. Like any other sport shoes, it is best to try them on before making a purchase. A knowledgeable golf store employee should be able to give you advice on quality, durability, and price.

You should also consider carrying an umbrella on the course. Depending on your geographical location, it may often rain when you are playing. To keep dry and comfortable, an umbrella is necessary, preferably a windproof golf umbrella. These umbrellas have large canopies so you can keep yourself and your golf bag dry during a downpour. Windproof umbrellas have a vent near the top so wind can escape the canopy and not bend or break the umbrella.

If your hands sweat easily, are soft, or are easily irritated, you may want to consider wearing a golf glove. The glove is worn on the target-side hand on all full swing shots to provide a better grip. Wearing a glove is a matter of personal preference.

Additional accessories we suggest you put in your golf bag include a mark repair tool to fix ball marks on the green, tees for teeing your ball, and sunscreen.

SCORING

Success in golf is measured by the number of strokes it takes you to move the ball from the teeing ground into the hole; the fewer strokes, the better the player. In a round of golf, the count begins on the first tee and ends when the ball drops in the 18th hole. One stroke is counted each time you attempt to strike the ball whether you make contact or not.

Every golf course has a par rating. Par represents the strokes a highly competent player would need to complete all 18 holes. As mentioned, each hole on the golf course has a par rating, and the totaled par ratings of all 18 holes are the par rating for the course.

Par-3 holes are short because the highly competent golfer should reach the green from the tee box in one stroke and then take two putts to complete the hole. Par-4 holes require two shots to reach the green, one from the tee box to the fairway and one from the fairway to the green. Par-5 holes allow for three strokes from the tee box to the green. The typical 18-hole golf course is comprised of 4 par-3 holes, 10 par-4 holes, and 4 par-5 holes, for a course par of 72.

Golf has terminology to describe how you played each hole relative to par. If you took one stroke from the tee box to hole out the ball (this normally occurs only on par 3s), this is called an *ace* or a *hole-in-one*. If your score on a hole is two under par, this is called an *eagle*. Both the ace and the eagle are rare occurrences. One under par on a hole is a *birdie* and a prized score. It is common for beginning and intermediate players

to shoot scores that are over par. One over par is a *bogey*, two over par is a *double bogey*, three over is a *triple bogey*, and so on.

How you play a hole and where your ball lands affects your score. If your ball stops in the fairway on your tee shot, this is called a *fairway hit*. If you put the ball on the green in the allocated number of strokes (on a par 3, that would be one stroke), you are said to have reached the *green in regulation*. If you miss the green but are able to chip or pitch the ball on the green and then hole the ball out with one putt, this is called an *up and down*. An up and down from a green-side bunker is called a *sand save*. *Number of putts* represents your putting proficiency. Par is 36 putts. If you hit fewer putts than that, you are considered a good putter. These terms are important indicators of your success as a golfer; the greater your proficiency in any of these areas, the better golfer you are. In step 12 you will see the part these aspects of the game should play in your practice routines.

KEEPING A SCORECARD

When you check in for your tee time, you will be provided with a scorecard for the course (figure 4). The scorecard will list the holes, the par for each hole, the distance from each set of tee boxes to the hole, and the handicap for each hole. The handicap indicates the difficulty of the hole in comparison to the other holes on the course. The hole with the lowest number (1) is the most difficult and the hole with the highest number (18) is the least difficult. Also listed on the scorecard are the course rating and slope. These numbers indicate the course difficulty in comparison to other courses. A course with a higher rating is more difficult than a course with a lower rating. For example, a course with a rating of 70.6/132 is more difficult than a course with a rating of 67.6/121.

Although the scorecard provides information regarding the course and the holes, its primary purpose is for you to record your score in stroke play. As you play a round, write down the number of strokes you took for each hole, including penalty strokes. Most players simply

write down the number of strokes, but some players prefer to add a bit more information. For example, if you score a birdie on the hole (one under par for the hole), you circle the number you record. If you eagle the hole (two under par), you circle the number twice. A bogie (one over par) is indicated by drawing a box around the number. A double bogie number receives two boxes, a triple bogie receives three boxes, and so on.

It is customary in tournament play for players to swap scorecards and keep the score of their opponent. In recreational play, players can keep their own score or one member of the group can keep the scores for everyone on a single card.

A word of caution: When playing a tournament, carefully check the hole-by-hole score and the final score. If you sign the scorecard and turn it in to tournament officials and it is later discovered that you signed an incorrect scorecard, you will be automatically disqualified from the tournament. In 1968, Roberto De Vicenzo had apparently won one of the most prestigious

HOLE	1	2	3	4	5	6	7	8	9	OUT	10	11	12	13	14	15	16	17	18	IN	TOT	HCP	NET
GOLD	402	495	428	197	450	182	445	406	522	3527	400	451	210	510	229	381	405	548	456	3590	7117	M74.5/136	
BLUE	368	487	398	169	427	176	410	382	507	3324	388	401	186	500	189	367	368	535	400	3334	6658	M72.1/130	
WHITE	337	471	370	145	405	160	380	353	477	3098	363	370	164	487	160	345	331	506	390	3116	6214	M70.4/125	
GREEN	315	439	348	117	391	132	353	322	432	2849	354	347	149	462	124	315	305	426	346	2828	5677	M67.8/115	
PAR	4	5	4	3	4	3	4	4	5	36	4	4	3	5	3	4	4	5	4	36	72	HCP	NET
HANDICAP	5	11	13	15	3	17	1	7	9		14	12	16	2	18	10	6	8	4				
										INITIAL													
GREEN	315	439	348	117	391	132	353	322	432	2849	354	347	149	462	124	315	305	426	346	2828	5677	W72.8/131	
RED	294	405	316	98	354	107	348	289	417	2628	329	313	126	415	112	273	275	421	325	2589	5217	W70.6/123	
PAR	4	5	4	3	4	3	4	4	5	36	4	4	3	5	3	4	4	5	4	36	72		
HANDICAP	3	9	1	15	5	17	11	13	7		8	12	16	2	18	10	14	6	4				

DATE _____ SCORER _____ ATTEST _____

Figure 4 Sample scorecard.

tournaments in golf, the Masters, until it was discovered that he had inadvertently signed an incorrect scorecard and was disqualified. If your score is supposed to count, be sure to count it carefully!

BASIC RULES

The fundamental goal of golf is to get the ball in each hole on the course in the fewest number of strokes. The rules of the game provide a framework that regulates what a player can and cannot do in this quest. The rules permit fair and impartial competition between players and with the course (we play against par). The better you understand the rules, the better you understand golf and the more enjoyment you can derive from the game.

The rules of golf are often defined in terms of the penalties a player incurs for certain actions and events on the course. Violation of a rule results in a one- or two-stroke penalty or a disqualification. The rules also provide options for certain course conditions. The rules specify a player's actions when preparing to strike the ball, conditions surrounding the ball at rest, and course conditions not under a player's control.

The rules of golf are intended to maintain the integrity of the game. As a golfer, you are expected to know the rules and follow them. If you are uncertain of a rule, you may ask your playing partners or opponents to state the rules. At all times, you must abide by the rules; otherwise you are not playing golf.

As you will see in the following rules, in many situations you must replay a ball from its original position. If you believe your ball may be lost, in a hazard, or out of bounds, you may declare your belief that your ball is unplayable and hit a provisional ball, which you hit from the original spot in case your first ball must be returned under the rules. This courtesy is intended to keep the pace of play by not making a player walk back on the course. If, after hitting the provisional ball, you discover that your first ball is playable, you can pick up the provisional ball and play with your original ball. If the first ball is unplayable, declare it so and play your provisional ball as the ball in play, assessing the required penalty.

In this section we will review the key rules of stroke play, the most common scoring system, and typical situations that occur in a round of golf. However, as you get more serious about the game, particularly if you are going to be competitive, you need to familiarize yourself with the rules of golf as established and published by the United States Golf Association (USGA) (www.usga.org).

Relief and Free Drops

On the golf course, the ball may come to rest in certain situations that are beyond your control and therefore result in no penalty. In such cases, you may elect to play the ball as it lies (always an option in golf), or seek relief from the obstruction with a free drop. The latter option allows you to relocate the ball fairly (figure 5).

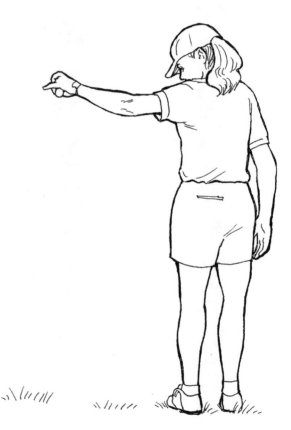

Figure 5 Free drop.

To exercise the free-drop option, you must stand outside the trouble area at the closest point where an unencumbered strike at the ball is possible. At this point, you raise the ball to shoulder height, extend your arm, and drop the ball within one club length of your spot. The ball must come to rest no closer to the hole than the original spot from which you are seeking relief.

Conditions from which you are entitled to seek relief include but are not limited to the following:

- Ground under repair (usually marked with a sign or white paint)
- Man-made objects embedded in the course such as paved cart paths, sprinkler heads, and metal grates
- Holes made by burrowing animals
- Casual water (water not normally on the course) left by rain or sprinklers
- Staked trees or shrubs

One-Stroke Penalties

Some situations result in a one-stroke penalty. For a one-stroke penalty, one stroke is added to your score even though you did not strike at the ball. Further procedures govern how you continue play once you have been assessed the penalty.

- **Lost ball.** If you cannot find your ball after a five-minute search, the ball is declared lost and you must strike another ball from the spot at which you struck the original ball, with a one-stroke penalty. This is known as loss of stroke and distance.
- **Out of bounds.** If your shot passes the white stakes on the perimeter of a golf course, it has gone out of bounds (OB). If any portion of the ball lies inbounds, the ball is considered inbounds. Like a lost ball, the penalty for OB is loss of stroke and distance. You play the next shot from the place of the previous shot, with a one-stroke penalty.
- **Direct water hazard.** A water hazard marked by yellow stakes is a direct water hazard. If your ball comes to rest inside the yellow stakes, you have three options. First, you may play the ball as it lies with no penalty stroke assessed, although your club cannot touch any object within the hazard until you initiate your swing to strike the ball or you will be assessed a one-stroke penalty. Second, you may replay the ball from the previous spot from which it was struck, with a one-stroke penalty. Third, keeping in line with the point at which the ball entered the hazard and the hole, you may back away from the hole as far as desired and drop the ball, with a one-stroke penalty.

- **Lateral water hazard.** A water hazard marked with red stakes is a lateral water hazard. Lateral water hazards normally run parallel to the course. You have four options if your ball comes to rest within a lateral water hazard. First, you may play the ball as it lies with no penalty as long as your club does not contact any object within the hazard until you make a fair strike at the ball. Second, you may return to the original location of the shot and replay the stroke, with a one-stroke penalty. Third, you may determine where the ball entered the hazard and, with a one-stroke penalty, drop a ball within two club lengths of this spot, no closer to the hole. Fourth, you may go to the far side of the hazard directly across from where the ball entered. Keeping the hole and the point of hazard entry on line, drop a ball as far as desired and in line with the hole and point of entry, again with a one-stroke penalty.
- **Unplayable lie.** If you determine that a ball is unplayable, for example if it is against a tree or under a thick bush, you may declare it unplayable and assess yourself a one-stroke penalty. Now you have three options. First, you may replay the ball from the original spot. Second, you may drop the ball within two club lengths of the spot in which it came to rest. Third, you may go back as far as desired to drop the ball on a line from the hole through the unplayable point.

- **Accidentally moving the ball.** When a ball has been struck from the tee but not yet holed out, if you move the ball from its original position while it is in play, you must return it to the original position and take a one-stroke penalty. If you fail to return the ball to the original point of play, you are assessed a two-stroke penalty.

Two-Stroke Penalties

Some situations result in a two-stroke penalty, in which two strokes are added to your score even though you do not strike at the ball. Additional procedures govern how you continue play once you have been assessed the penalty.

- **Grounding the club in a hazard.** If your club touches the ground or any object affixed to the ground (for example, a tree or a post) while in a hazard (for example, a water hazard or sand bunker) before you initiate a swing, you are assessed a two-stroke penalty.

- **Playing the wrong ball.** If you strike a ball that is not the ball in play, you are assessed a two-stroke penalty and must find your own ball and continue play. It is appropriate for players to mark their golf balls for the purpose of identification. You may not alter the playability of the ball as you mark it. A waterproof marker works best, and it is customary to use a line, symbol, dots, or initials as markers. PGA tour player Duffy Waldorf has his children draw pictures and symbols on the balls he plays in tournaments, making it easy to spot his ball on the golf course.

- **Striking the flag or another ball when putting from on the green.** If you play a ball from the putting green and your ball strikes either the flag stick or another player's ball, you are assessed a two-stroke penalty. You should play the next stroke where your ball came to rest but return your opponent's ball to its original location. It is your responsibility to have the flag tended or removed before playing a ball from the putting green. There is no penalty if you hit the flag stick when shooting the ball from off the green. If you believe your opponent's ball lies within your putting line, ask your opponent to mark the placement of the ball with a small object and remove the ball from the green.

- **Asking advice.** If you are playing a competitive round, you may not ask for any advice that will aid your play, such as which club to play or how to swing. You may, however, ask for general course information such as the location of yardage markers or the hole. This rule would not apply if you were receiving on-course instruction and were not planning to use your score for a competition or for handicap purposes.

Disqualification

You can be disqualified, or not have your score count in a competition, if you play the wrong ball and do not correct the error before teeing off on the next hole. As mentioned, scoring errors also may result in disqualification. Scoring errors usually result from recording an incorrect score on a particular hole. If you incur a penalty on a hole and do not assess yourself for that penalty, you have recorded an incorrect score and could be disqualified.

ETIQUETTE

The rich history of golf has left a legacy of social protocol that will enhance your enjoyment and improve playing conditions. No penalties are assessed for violating the rules of etiquette, but such offenses are considered rude. By following the rules of etiquette, you allow all golfers to enjoy the game and you send the message that you understand the sport. Most of the golfers you meet on a course won't be concerned about your skill level, but they will be concerned if you do not exhibit the social graces of the sport. Following are 10 keys to etiquette on the golf course.

10 Keys to Courtesy

1. Play in a group. If the starter places you with another group, take advantage of the opportunity to get to know other golfers.
2. Keep your tee time. Tee off in the correct order.
3. Follow the correct order of play.
4. On the green, follow the correct order of play, mark your ball, and tend the flag. Do not stand or walk in a putting player's line of sight, target line, or line of return. Remain quiet and still when another player is putting.
5. Maintain an appropriate pace of play. Be ready to play your shot when it is your turn and let faster groups play through.
6. Maintain the golf course.
7. Be safety conscious.
8. Operate the golf cart correctly.
9. Dress appropriately for the course, following the course's dress code.
10. Be courteous to your opponents, other golfers, and those who take care of the course.

Group Play

A round of golf is traditionally played in groups of two, three, or four, known as twosomes, threesomes, or foursomes. You may play alone, but group play is the norm. If you show up at a golf course alone, the starter may place you with another group. Consider it an opportunity to get to know other golfers.

Tee Time

It is traditional to schedule a tee time by calling the golf course within a week of the round you intend to play. You will be scheduled a time to start your round, at which time you are expected to be on the course striking your first shot off the first tee. Come to the course up to an hour before your tee time so you can make sure you have all the equipment you need, check in with the starter, and warm up by stroking some putts on the practice green and hitting some balls on the practice range.

The first person to tee off is said to have the honors. On the first hole, guests usually have the honors; otherwise, a flip of the coin can determine honors. For every hole after the first, the honor goes to the player who scored the lowest on the previous hole. If two golfers had the same score on the previous hole, the honor carries over from the previous hole.

Order of Play

After all golfers tee off, the distance each ball is to the hole determines the order of play. The player whose ball is farthest from the hole hits first. The other golfers should remain behind the player until the shot is struck. The golfers then continue to the next farthest ball from the hole. After a hole is finished, the order of play at the next hole is determined by score, from lowest to highest.

On the Green

Etiquette on the green is particularly important due to the proximity of other players and the number of activities taking place. Rules and etiquette ensure that players can attend to their business fairly and without undue delay.

The order of putting is similar to the order of play from the fairway. The player farthest from the hole is the next player to putt. This applies whether all players are on the green or not. For example, if one player is 20 feet (6 meters) from the hole and on the green and another is 10 feet (3 meters) from the hole but in the green-side rough, the player farthest away has the honors, in this case the player on the green. However, the group would typically give the player in the rough the option to play first so that all players are on the green before putting begins. The player in the rough can decide whether to play onto the green or wait.

It is common courtesy to mark your ball once you reach the green. This will be explained in greater depth in step 1, but briefly, marking your ball means placing a small object such as a coin behind your ball and removing your ball from the green until it is your turn to putt.

If one of your playing partners has a putt that is so long it is difficult for him to see the hole, it is courtesy to tend the flag. Tending the flag requires a player to stand beside the hole with one hand on the flag stick, allowing the putting player to easily see the hole. After the putt is struck, the flag tender removes the flag so that the putting player won't be assessed a two-stroke penalty for hitting the flag. A golfer playing a shot from off the green has the option of removing the flag or letting it remain in the hole, as there is no penalty for striking the flag with a ball played from off the green.

Several rules of etiquette determine where, or more precisely, where not, to stand or walk on the green. First, you should not stand in a putting player's line of sight during a putt. The line of sight is the area where the putter can immediately view the ball and the hole as well as directly behind the ball and beyond the hole. Standing in another player's line of sight is considered poor sporting behavior because it distracts the player. When another player is putting, or taking any stroke for that matter, you should remain quiet and still.

Second, you should not walk on your opponent's target line or line of return. The target line is the potential path the ball will roll on the green. The line of return is the line the ball will likely follow should it go past the hole and need to be putted back to the hole. Because greens are sensitive, they are susceptible to being scuffed, and footprints leave small depressions. These marks can unfairly deflect a well-struck putt away from the hole.

Pace of Play

Pace of play refers to the amount of time it takes to play a round of golf. On most courses, pace of play can take three and a half to four and a half hours depending on the length of the course and its difficulty. You can do several things to keep the pace of play going without rushing your preparation for or execution of a shot.

First, always be ready to play your shot when it is your turn. Because order of play is determined by the ball farthest from the hole, you should always know when it is your turn. Begin to plan your shot as you approach the ball and while your opponents are hitting their shots so that you know what shot you want to play and have the club in your hand when it is your turn. Don't rush your swing, but be quick to get to your ball. Do as much preparation as possible before your turn. If socializing is an important part of the game for you, do so while walking to your shot, but be prepared to play when it is your turn. Most golfers do not mind playing with a beginner, but they do mind playing with someone who is unprepared when it is time to play and thus slows play down.

Once you complete a hole, leave the green quickly so that it is open for the group behind you. Record your score while walking to the next tee. Once you reach the next tee, determine who has honors and hit your tee shots.

There will be times when a group behind you is playing more quickly than your group. If you notice the group behind you has to wait for you to finish before they can play their shots and no one is in front of you, it is courtesy to let them play through. For example, if someone in your group has lost a ball and you're going to take time to look for it, consider waving the group behind you through. Once you wave them through, stand aside the fairway or far from the green so that they can play their shots without interference. This is an important courtesy that keeps the pace of play up for everyone.

Maintain the Golf Course

Imagine walking to your ball in a bunker and seeing it deep in someone else's footprint. Or, imagine seeing a large ball mark between your ball and the hole. In either case, you would naturally feel you were being disadvantaged by someone else's lack of courtesy. If the player before you had raked the bunker or repaired the ball mark, you would have a considerably better shot. Because we all play the golf course, we must all take part in maintaining it so that those who come after us find the course in the best condition possible. You should expect no less and give no less.

On the green, be particularly careful to leave the putting surface as smooth as possible. When removing the flag from the hole, be careful to place it on the green; do not drop it. Take care as you walk so as not to harm the grass. Place your golf bag and other equipment off the green. Always repair any ball marks you make when hitting the green. To repair a ball mark, insert a tee or ball-mark repair tool into the ground around the mark and lift the ground back to its original level. Then tap down uneven areas with your putter.

On the fairway, replace any divots you make when striking your ball, or fill them with sand if it is provided on a golf cart. To replace a divot, pick up the piece of grass and soil unit that you cut from the ground with your club, return it to the bare spot, and step down on it (figure 6).

Figure 6 Replacing a divot on the fairway.

Bunkers also need particular care since you must play the ball as it lies. Be sure you leave the bunker looking as well as you found it, if not better. Rake any ball marks and footprints you may have made. Rake a bunker by walking backward out of it, gently covering your marks as you leave (figure 7). Return the rake to a safe area with the spikes turned down.

Figure 7 Raking the bunker.

Be Safety Conscious

Fortunately, few injuries occur in golf, in part because golfers take care of the two sources of danger they carry with them—clubs and balls. Be certain the area is clear before you swing a golf club, especially when you take warm-up swings, as others may not be aware that you are about to swing the club. Also, know where your golf ball and the golf balls of your partners are located. Don't play a shot if there is a danger of hitting someone. If you hit a shot that looks as if it might strike someone, loudly yell "Fore!" (as in, "Be forewarned"). Don't be embarrassed to yell this warning; everyone hits an errant shot from time to time. People on a golf course expect an errant shot every now and again, but they also expect and deserve an appropriate warning.

Cart Operation

Golf carts are a common fixture on golf courses today. While walking a beautiful course is the best option, sometimes that option simply isn't available. When operating a golf cart, drive the cart only where allowed, and never drive on or near a green. Park the cart where it will not interfere with another player's shot or line of sight. If you are required to leave the cart on the cart path, take as many clubs as you think you may need for the shot and perhaps a few more, because walking back to the cart to retrieve more clubs will slow the pace of play. If you are sharing a cart, drive it to a place that is mutually convenient for both players to play their shots.

Look Like a Player

Most golf courses have a dress code, and playing the course requires you to adhere to the code. In general, dress code is slacks or dress shorts, golf skirts, golf shirts, and soft-spiked shoes or tennis shoes. The last point is particularly important, as street shoes or heavy-soled shoes can damage the greens. When in doubt, dress conservatively and neatly. Dress for success!

Golf With Courtesy

Good sporting behavior is a fundamental principle of golf. Golf is the only sport in which even at the highest levels players call penalties on themselves; there are no referees. Courtesy should be present in every part of your game. Make no mistake, you can retain decorum and courtesy and still be highly competitive.

Golf courtesy begins with the way you treat your playing partners. Be quiet and still when they play their shots. Don't get in another player's line of sight, and don't allow your shadow to fall on another player's ball or on the line on which another player is putting. If a player leaves equipment near you, return it to the right person. Tend the flag when necessary or hand a player a rake for the bunker if you are close. The same courtesies will be returned to you.

You should also be courteous to players not in your group. Keep loud noise to a minimum, as someone in a group near you may be playing a shot. Maintain the course and the pace of play. When necessary, let others play through.

Finally, show courtesy to the people operating the golf course. A simple "Please" and "Thank you" will show your respect and appreciation. Masters Champion Phil Mickelson is renowned for his kindness and expressions of appreciation for the people who organize and conduct the tournaments and golf courses he plays. He simply treats others as he himself would like to be treated.

Golf has a rich and rewarding heritage. Few sports are played in settings so natural or lovely. Golf can be enjoyed by the young and old, and it is one of the few sports in which people from all walks of life can play together regardless of age or ability. Golf is a game for a lifetime.

Now that you have been introduced to the basics of the golf course, scoring, equipment, rules, and etiquette, we will turn our attention to developing your skills and deepening your knowledge. In the following chapters, you will take several steps to golf success. Whether you have never touched a club before or have been playing for several years, these steps will help you gain a level of skill and confidence that will help you find golf an enjoyable and rewarding game.

Putting the Ball Into the Hole

Commit this maxim to memory: *Successful golf is getting the ball into the hole in the least number of strokes*. Developing a beautiful swing, hitting a long drive, or having the latest equipment means little if high numbers appear next to your name on the scorecard. If success is what you seek, it makes sense to begin with the skill that is most responsible for getting the ball in the hole—putting.

If you are not a good putter, you will never be a successful golfer. Harvey Penick, one of the greatest golf teachers of all time, once wrote, "Golf should be learned starting at the cup and progressing back toward the tee . . . If a beginner tries to learn the game at the tee and move on toward the green, postponing the short game until last, this is one beginner who will be lucky ever to beat anybody." Learning to putt is the first step to becoming a successful golfer.

A putt can be made with any club in your bag, but the putter is designed specifically for this stroke. Putters come in many shapes and sizes, so it is best to experiment with various putters to determine which one leads to the best results. For most players, a traditional putter works well, and it is a good place for beginners to start.

Unlike other shots in golf, the putt is intended to roll along the ground and never become airborne. To accommodate this, the putter has a near-vertical face with little or no angle. Also, of all the shots in golf, the putt is struck with the least amount of force. Traditional putters have short shafts to generate slower, more controllable clubhead speed.

PUTTING RULES AND ETIQUETTE

There are two rules and several points of etiquette for the putting green. The first rule allows you to lift your ball once it has come to rest on the green (rule 16.1B). Once you lift the ball, you may clean it if you so desire. You must, however, return the ball to the spot from which it was lifted. Failure to return the ball to its original location results in a two-stroke penalty.

To mark the location of this spot, place a small coin or similar object behind the ball before lifting it (figure 1.1). You should also mark your ball if it interferes with another player's putting line. Once the ball is clean, you may return it to its original spot on the green and remove the marker before stroking your putt.

Figure 1.1 Marking the ball on the green.

The second rule states that when playing a ball from the putting green, your ball must not hit the flag or flagstick (rule 17.3) or another player's ball at rest on the putting green (rule 19.5A). Should you strike the flag, flagstick, or another player's ball at rest on the green while putting, you incur a penalty of two strokes. It is your responsibility to have the flag or an opponent's ball removed if there is any chance your putt may strike it. This rule applies only if your ball has come to rest on the putting green. Hitting the flag, flagstick, or another player's ball with a stroke taken from off the putting green results in no penalty. Play your ball from wherever it came to rest off the green; if you hit another player's ball on the green, that player simply replaces the ball where it was before it was struck.

It is proper etiquette for the player who is farthest from the hole to putt first. Continue putting the ball farthest from the hole until all players have holed out. It is also proper etiquette for the player closest to the flag to remove the flag from the hole before anyone putts. Be careful to not scuff the green with your shoes or leave deep depressions with your steps or equipment. Damage to the greens caused by carelessness will affect the quality of play for the golfers who follow you, and due to the sensitive nature of the grass, it can take a long time for the greens to heal.

Etiquette on the green requires you to avoid walking or standing on another player's line of play. The line of play is an imaginary line that extends from the ball to the hole as well as beyond both the ball and the hole. Walking where other players must roll their ball to the hole creates depressions on the target line at best and leaves spike marks at worst. According to the rules, a player cannot fix spike marks before putting, so it is unfair and discourteous to create such a situation. Standing on the line of play, either behind the ball or behind the hole, while another player is putting may distract that player. As your partners line up and stroke their putts, stay well to the side of their line of play.

The first player to hole a ball replaces the flag when all players have holed out. Before leaving the green, etiquette requires you to repair any marks made by your ball when it hit the green or any other marks in your vicinity (figure 1.2). Ball marks are repaired using a tee or a ball-mark repair tool, an inexpensive tool for repairing indentations in the green. Push the tee or tool into the ground alongside the indentation and push the ground toward the center of the indentation, continuing until you have gone completely around the ball mark. With your putter head, tamp down the spot until it is smooth. This will leave the green smooth for the next player and help the green heal more quickly from being struck by your ball. Good etiquette suggests that you repair your ball mark and at least one more mark that might have been left by another player.

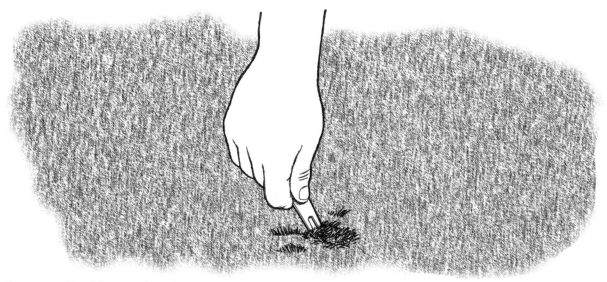

Figure 1.2   Repairing a mark on the green.

EXECUTING THE PUTT

The first step of the putting stroke is lightly gripping the putter in the palms of your hands. To create an efficient and controlled stroke, the hands should be directly opposite each other, as if you were clapping (figure 1.3a). Next, set the putter face behind the ball so that it is square to the target line, the line you intend your ball to track along to the target. Assume a comfortable posture in which you feel relaxed. Your arms and hands should be under your shoulders, your eyes directly over the ball, your knees slightly bent, and your weight evenly distributed over both feet. To allow for a straight putt, your shoulders, hips, knees, and feet should be parallel with the target line. The ball should be slightly closer to the target side of the center of your stance.

The putting stroke is a pendulum action, much like the swing of the pendulum at the bottom of a large grandfather clock. Using a rocking action with the shoulders, bring the putter back and then forward through the ball with an even tempo (figure 1.3b). The arms and wrist have very little independent movement in a good putting stroke. Bring the putter back approximately the same distance as you bring it forward, just like the pendulum on a clock. The length of the stroke is directly related to the length of the putt: the longer the stroke, the longer the putt. A steady, rhythmic, straight-back and straight-through stroke helps bring the putter to the ball with the face of the putter directly facing the target line of the putt, allowing you to contact the ball squarely in the center of the putter, also known as the sweet spot.

A couple of key factors promote solid contact between the ball and putter. The first is a steady body. A player needs to be relaxed during the stroke, but there is very little movement in the lower body (no weight shift, little or no movement of the hips or legs), no lateral movement of the upper body, and little movement from the arms or wrists. The shoulders turning around a fixed spine provide almost all necessary movement. The angle of the spine should remain constant throughout the putting stroke.

The second key to a solid putt is light grip pressure. A light grip allows the shoulders, arms, and hands to respond naturally in the stroke without conscious thought. A light grip also keeps the putter on the target line longer because it gives you the feeling of stroking the ball into the hole rather than smacking the ball and hoping it ends up somewhere near the hole. Finally, maintaining a light grip on the putter makes it easier to relax the entire body and thus allows your natural muscle responses to help you putt successfully.

A final key to consistent, confident contact is a preshot routine. The preshot routine is discussed in more detail in step 11, but a few brief notes here will help you develop your putting skill. Simply put, a preshot routine is a series of activities you routinely perform before each stroke. A preshot routine includes picking your target (where you want the ball to go), identifying your target line (the path the ball will take to get to the target), setting up to stroke the ball, and stroking the ball along the target line to the target. These actions are linked in a continuous, relaxed flow. Most players select the target and target line while standing or squatting behind the ball because this provides a better view of the green. After picking the target and line, step up to the ball, place your putter head behind the ball along the target line, assume your putting address position, look at the hole, look at the ball, and stroke your putt. No single routine is applicable to every golfer, so you will need to experiment a bit to find the routine that fits you best. To ingrain a preshot putting routine, you need to practice it on the practice green. The preshot routine drill (see page 6) will help you develop this vital part of your putting stroke.

After the putter strokes the ball, several keys in the follow-through help ensure a successful putt. First, the wrists should be locked or firm as the putter head comes through the ball all the way to the finish (figure 1.3c). This promotes square contact with the ball during impact. Flipping or moving the wrists changes the angle of the putter head, making solid contact difficult to achieve. The putter head should accelerate through the ball—it is a stroke, not a strike. Finally, if the putt is made with a rhythmic stroke, the follow-through will be the same length as the backstroke.

While different players have different putting styles, many good players keep their heads still and don't even look up to watch the ball after they stroke it. This helps them maintain a steady body during the stroke. The great South African player and noted putter Bobby Locke offered the following advice to aspiring players: "Listen for the ball to fall into the hole; don't watch it." Not only does listening to the ball fall promote good putting technique, it is a sweet sound every golfer likes to hear.

Figure 1.3   Executing the Putt

PREPARATION

1. Turn the palms toward each other
2. Square the putter head to the target line
3. Square the shoulders and hips to the target line
4. Set feet shoulder-width apart and evenly distribute your weight
5. Eyes are over the ball
6. Exert light grip pressure

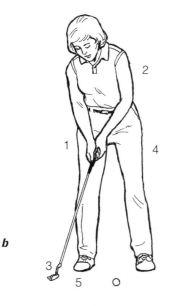

b

c

EXECUTION

1. Move the shoulders, arms, and hands as one unit
2. Move the shoulders in a pendulum motion
3. Putter head should come back along the target line
4. Keep the lower body still
5. Backswing and forward swing should be the same distance and tempo

FOLLOW-THROUGH

1. Putter head should come through and follow along the target line
2. Keep the wrists firm throughout the swing (no breaking)
3. Putter head should come through the ball at the same tempo as the backswing
4. Listen rather than watch for the ball to fall into the cup

Misstep

On straight putts, the ball consistently misses left or right.

Correction

This misstep may be caused by body misalignment. Check to ensure that feet, thighs, hips, and shoulders are all parallel with the target line. Try the two clubs drill (page 7). Another cause might be that the putter's face is not square at impact. The putter head must track along the target line at the point of impact. Try the target line drill (page 7).

Putting Stroke Drill 1. *Preshot Routine*

A consistent preshot routine will increase your confidence and improve your consistency. For this drill, take one ball onto the practice green and practice a preshot routine to different golf holes. Vary the distance for each putt and attempt to follow the same routine for each putt. Repeat 10 times.

Success Check

- Stand behind the ball to determine the target and target line.
- Take a few practice strokes, if desired.

Score Your Success

Consistent preshot routine = 1 point per hole

Make the putt = 1 point per hole

Your score ___

Putting Stroke Drill 2. *Pendulum Progression*

The putting stroke is a pendulum action with the shoulders providing the power to the arms, hands, and putter, which work as a unit like a pendulum. This drill is designed to ingrain this important action.

Without a putter, assume a putting posture with the palms of both hands lightly pressed together directly over a ball. Rock your shoulders, letting the arms and hands swing back and forth over the ball in a straight line about 3 feet (.9 meters) long. If done correctly, the wrists should stay firm and your spine angle should not change.

Repeat the drill with a putter but remove the ball. Grip pressure should be light and the arms, hands, and putter should function as one unit. Concentrate on creating pendulum-like strokes, with the putter moving in a straight, 3-foot line. Maintain your spine angle and firm wrists.

Once you feel comfortable with both parts of the progression, you are ready to score yourself. Repeat the first part of the progression (ball and no putter), but place two ball markers on a putting green approximately 2 feet (.6 meters) apart. Attempt 10 strokes, giving yourself 1 point every time your hands pass over the ball and both markers when you stroke. Repeat the second part of the progression (putter and no ball). Attempt 10 strokes, giving yourself 1 point every time your putter passes over the ball and both markers when you stroke.

To Decrease Difficulty

- Without a putter, stand with one foot back and move arms and hands in a 2-foot line over the ball.
- With a putter but without a ball, stand with one foot back and move the putter in a 2-foot line.

To Increase Difficulty

- Place two tees 3 feet apart on the practice green. Repeat both parts of the progression, passing over or touching the tees on each stroke.
- Repeat both parts of the progression with your eyes closed to develop a feel for the pendulum action.

Success Check

- Keep the back and forward swings the same length.
- Arms, hands, and putter should act as a single unit.
- Don't break the wrists on the stroke.
- Keep the lower body still during the entire stroke.

Score Your Success

Hands pass over the ball and both markers = 1 point each time

Putter passes over both markers = 1 point each time

Your score ___

Putting Stroke Drill 3. *Target Line*

To stroke a putt into the hole, you must be able to identify and putt along a target line. The target line is the path the ball will follow as it rolls across the green and into the hole. This drill will help you take a stance that allows you to see your target line as you putt.

Place a ball 3 feet from a hole on a practice green. Align the small lettering or brand name on the golf ball so that it is pointing at the hole. The lettering should be directly over the target line. This will help you identify the target line when you take your stance over the ball. Set the center of your putter head directly behind the ball lettering and then stroke the putt, attempting to drive the center of your putter head through the lettering on the ball. Repeat 10 times.

Repeat the drill, this time taking your stance over the ball in preparation for stroking a putt after positioning the ball. Hold the putter in your dominant hand and an extra ball in your other hand. Place the putter head behind the ball along the target line and take your normal putting posture. Place the extra golf ball on the bridge of your nose

between your eyes and drop the golf ball. If your eyes are aligned properly over the ball, the ball you dropped should strike the ball on the green. Repeat 10 times.

To Increase Difficulty

- Repeat the first part of the drill with the ball 10 to 15 feet (3 to 4.5 meters) from the hole.

Success Check

- Maintain your spine angle throughout each stroke.
- Keep the body in balance.

Score Your Success

Make the putt with the ball 3 feet from the hole = 1 point each time

Dropped ball hits the ball on the green = 1 point each time

Your score ___

Putting Stroke Drill 4. *Two Clubs*

A consistent club path leads to better directional control. Place two clubs parallel with each other on the ground with the grip ends alongside a hole on the practice putting green (figure 1.4). The clubs should be a little farther apart than the length of the putter head. Practice a pendulum-like putting action with the putter head remaining square to the hole and moving between the clubs without touching them. Do not use a ball at first. Repeat 10 times.

To Decrease Difficulty

- Try to keep every other stroke from touching the clubs on the ground.

To Increase Difficulty

- Place a ball between the clubs, approximately 3 feet from the hole. Repeat the drill, attempting to clear the clubs and putt the ball into the hole. Repeat 10 times.

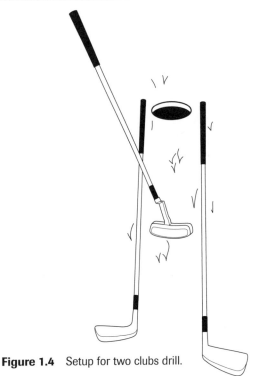

Figure 1.4 Setup for two clubs drill.

- Complete the drill with your eyes closed, first without and then with a ball. Repeat 10 times with the ball.
- Remove the clubs and draw a line from 6 feet (1.8 meters) away to the hole using carpenter's chalk. Make the putter head follow this line on the backswing and forward swing. Place a golf ball on this line and putt the ball along the line into the hole.

Success Check

- Length of backward and forward swings should be the same.
- Make a rocking motion with the shoulders to create pendulum action.
- Keep the wrists firm throughout the entire stroke.

Score Your Success

Stroke between two clubs as if putting, no ball, putter head doesn't touch either club = 1 point each stroke

Stroke between two clubs, putting with a ball 3 feet from the hole, make the putt, putter head doesn't touch either club = 1 point each made putt

Stroke between two clubs, putting with a ball 3 feet from the hole, eyes closed, make the putt, putter head doesn't touch either club = 1 point each made putt

Your score ___

Putting Stroke Drill 5. *Distance Control*

The ability to control the distance you putt a ball is vital to your success as a putter. Putts struck too hard or too lightly not only have no chance to go in the hole, they often make the second putt far more difficult than it would have been if the ball had come to rest near the hole.

Three factors influence the distance a putted ball will travel: the solidness of the strike by the putter head, the length of the swing, and the slope of the green (downhill putts obviously will roll farther than uphill putts if all other factors are equal). This drill will help you develop distance control. Pay particular attention to the length of the swing and the influence of the green's slope on the distance the ball travels.

Place three balls on the putting green (figure 1.5). Select three different holes. One hole should be a short distance away (3 feet or fewer), one hole a medium distance (6 to 12 feet), and one hole a longer distance (15 feet or more). Putt the balls in order from closest to farthest holes. Walk to the first ball struck and continue putting until you hole the ball. Remove the ball and place it near the hole. Putt it to the medium-distance hole.

Figure 1.5 Setup for distance control drill.

Continue putting both the first ball and the second ball until both balls are holed, always putting the ball farthest from the hole first. Remove the two balls from the second hole and place them near the hole. Putt these balls to the farthest hole. Continue putting to this final hole until you hole all three balls.

To Decrease Difficulty

- Place three golf clubs at a distance of 3, 6, and 9 feet (1, 2, and 3 meters). Putt to the golf clubs instead of holes. Attempt to have the ball come to rest within 6 inches (15 centimeters) of the targeted golf club.
- Place three golf balls in the middle of the practice putting green. Putt to the fringe of the putting green, attempting to get the ball as close to the fringe as possible without the ball going off the green.

To Increase Difficulty

- Incorporate an uphill putt, a downhill putt, and a sidehill putt into the drill.
- Putt to tees placed into the putting green rather than holes. Place tees at short, medium, and long distances. The smaller targets make this variation more difficult.

- Listen for the ball to fall into the hole, not looking up to watch it.
- Putt to holes at distances of 10, 20, and 30 feet (3, 6, and 9 meters).

Success Check

- Backswing and forward swing should be the same distance on each stroke.
- Shoulders, arms, hands, and putter work together as a single unit.

Score Your Success

Count the total number of strokes you need to complete the drill.

27 putts or more = 0 points

21 to 26 putts = 5 points

15 to 20 putts = 10 points

11 to 14 putts = 15 points

10 putts or fewer = 20 points

Your score ___

Putting Stroke Drill 6. *Par-2 Golf Course*

Select nine holes on the practice putting green and order them 1 through 9. This is your par-2 golf course. You will putt to each hole in order from 1 to 9. Each hole has a par of 2 strokes. Once you have selected your course, place a ball approximately 6 feet from the first hole and putt the ball into the hole in as few strokes as possible. Remove the ball from the hole. Place it 3 feet from hole 2 and putt. Repeat until you have putted to all the holes. Count the total number of strokes you need to complete the round of 9 holes.

Success Check

- Use your best putting technique.

Score Your Success

More than 21 putts = 0 points

19 to 21 putts = 5 points

18 putts = 10 points

Fewer than 18 putts = 20 points

Your score ___

Putting Stroke Drill 7. *Ladder Drill*

Like drills 5 and 6, this drill develops distance control. Putt one ball from approximately 20 feet to within 1 foot (.3 meters) of the edge of the practice green. Putt the next ball along the same line so that it comes to rest 1 foot short of the previous putt (figure 1.6). Repeat until you have putted 10 balls.

To Decrease Difficulty

- Putt the first ball 10 feet and attempt to stroke each successive putt 1 foot short of the previous putt.

To Increase Difficulty

- Close your eyes just before putting the ball.
- Putt the first ball 10 feet and attempt to stroke each successive putt so that it just touches the previously putted ball.

Success Check

- Maintain your spine angle throughout the putt.
- Backswing and forward swing should be the same length.
- Do not move your head during the putting stroke.

Score Your Success

Give yourself 1 point if your first putt stops within 1 foot of the edge of the putting green. For every putt thereafter that comes within 1 foot of the previous putt without going past it, give yourself 1 point.

Your score ____

Figure 1.6 Ladder drill.

Putting Stroke Drill 8.   *Geometry Drills*

There are three geometry drills: line, circle, and triangle. For the line drill, place nine balls in a line, each ball 1 foot from the next with the first ball 1 foot from the hole. Begin with the ball closest to the hole and putt each ball in turn. Hole each ball before moving on to the next ball.

For the circle drill, place six balls in a circle 3 feet from the hole, six balls in a circle 6 feet from the hole, and six balls in a circle 9 feet from the hole (figure 1.7). Begin in the innermost circle. Putt the balls from the inner circle into the hole, working your way to the outermost circle. Hole each ball before moving to the next ball.

Figure 1.8   Triangle drill.

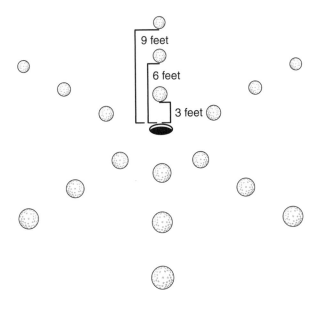

Figure 1.7   Circle drill.

For the triangle drill, create a triangle with three balls, each ball 2 feet (.6 meters) from the hole (figure 1.8). Use three more balls to create a second triangle, each ball 4 feet (1.2 meters) from the hole. Finally, create a third triangle with three balls, each ball 6 feet (1.8 meters) from the hole. Begin with the balls closest to the hole. Putt each ball in turn, working around the triangle. Hole each ball before moving on to the next ball.

To Decrease Difficulty

- Shorten the distance of the balls to the hole by 1 foot.

To Increase Difficulty

- Use a hole that has uphill, downhill, or sidehill undulation.
- Attempt to make all putts in all three drills consecutively. If you miss a putt, reset the line, circles, or triangles and begin again.

Success Check

- Keep the wrists firm on every stroke.

Score Your Success

Line drill: 1 point for each putt holed with a single stroke

Circle drill: 1 point for each putt holed with a single stroke

Triangle drill: 1 point for each putt holed with a single stroke; 1 additional point for every consecutive putt

Your score ___

READING THE GREEN

Again, the purpose of golf is to get the ball in the hole. As the ball sits on the putting green, bend or squat down behind the ball so you can see the ball, the green, and the hole. Next, imagine how the ball will roll along the putting surface and drop into the hole. In other words, determine how the ball will move from where it sits to the bottom of the cup. Figuring out how the putting surface will affect the roll of the ball is called reading the green.

When reading the green, try to answer three questions:

1. How fast does the ball need to go to just reach the hole?
2. In what direction does the ball need to start so the slope of the green will take the ball to the hole?
3. Do you need to hit a long putt or a short putt?

The first factor is pace, the second is line, and the third is putt length.

Pace

Pace is important because if you strike the ball too hard or too softly, it will stop long or short of the hole, resulting in a difficult second putt. With the right pace, the ball will finish close to, if not in, the hole. Pace is controlled by the length of the putting stroke. For a faster pace, increase the length of the backswing and forward swing. Remember, in a good putting stroke the length and speed of the backswing and forward swing are the same. Factors affecting pace include the slope of the green, the distance of the ball to the hole, and the type and length of grass.

Uphill putts must be struck with more force than when the surface is flat. Downhill putts must be struck with less force since gravity will increase the speed of the ball as it rolls. Obviously a longer putt requires more pace than a shorter putt.

If the grass is long, the putt will need more force. Conversely, closely mowed grass offers little resistance, so the putt should be struck with a lighter touch.

On most golf courses, practice greens near the first tee resemble the greens found on the golf course. Allow yourself a few minutes of putting practice before teeing off so you can get a feel for the pace the greens require for that particular day.

Misstep

You lack distance control; the ball rolls too far or not far enough.

Correction

You may not be keeping your wrists firm. If your wrists break during the stroke, the putter head will not consistently contact the ball solidly, causing a lack of distance control. Try the pendulum progression (page 6). Another cause might be uneven lengths of the backward and forward swings. Uneven tempo in the golf swing makes it difficult to consistently pace the ball. Try the two clubs drill, distance control drill, and ladder drill, beginning on page 7.

Line

Identifying the target line is important because the slope of the green affects the path the ball takes to the hole. Putting surfaces are not perfectly flat. The more undulation in the green, the more effect it has on the ball as the ball rolls to the hole.

Study the green to determine if the undulations will cause your ball to move left or right as it rolls toward the hole. If the slope of the green will move the ball from right to left, you need to start the ball to the right of the hole and let the natural slope feed the ball into the hole. The amount of left or right movement caused by the green is called *break* because the ball breaks from the direction in which it originally started. On greens that severely slope from left to right or right to left, play for more break.

To play for break, simply align the ball along the line you want to start the putt on rather than aligning the putt to the hole. Once you have aligned the ball, align your body along the same line. If necessary, take a practice stroke or two to get a feel for the pace needed to get the ball into the hole, and then concentrate on stroking the ball along the target line. If you read the green correctly, the ball will follow the target line and the slope of the green will carry the ball to the hole.

The pace of the ball will influence the target line because a slower ball is more affected by the slope than a faster ball. Good players know this and are keenly aware of the slope of the green near the hole because the ball will slow down as it approaches the hole.

Misstep

The ball breaks too little or too much as it approaches the hole.

Correction

If your ball is breaking wrong, you may be misreading the green. You need to understand how the slope of the green and the speed of the putt affect the roll of the ball. Try the hand-putting drill (page 14).

Putt Length

The length of the putt partly determines both the pace and the line you choose to play. Because the ball must travel a greater distance on a long putt, or lag putt, it will be more affected by the undulations of the green, which makes selecting and holding a line more difficult. Concentrate on the pace of long putts to ensure that your ball travels the proper distance to the hole. In other words, although the green undulation may cause the ball to go a little more to the left or right of the hole, proper pace will ensure that the ball does not finish too far from the hole.

Putts that are just a few feet from the hole are less affected by undulation because they do not have as far to travel. However, it is still possible for the green undulation to take the ball away from the hole if the putt is struck with insufficient pace. Aim short putts into the hole and putt with a bit more pace so that any undulation that exists will not deflect the ball from its target. This is known as putting the ball firm.

Strategic Putting Drill 1. *Hand-Putting*

If you were to follow a professional player's caddie on any pretournament practice round, you would see the caddie rolling golf balls by hand to different places on the green for every hole on the golf course. The caddie is learning the necessary line and pace for the most probable hole locations during the tournament. The tournament committee cuts the holes in different places on the green every day of the tournament, and this exercise allows the caddie to help the player determine the line and pace of the putt.

Hand-putting is an effective method for learning to read greens. To hand-putt, bend down at various places on the practice green and roll the ball with your hand to different holes (figure 1.9). Notice how the ball tracks differently to the hole when you change speed and direction (pace and line).

Next, from one position and using one hole, hand-putt the ball, changing the pace and line to determine which target line and pace offers the best chance for getting the ball into the hole. Select a hole that provides a moderate amount of break between you and the hole. You should be at least 10 feet from the hole. Hand-putt 10 balls.

Repeat the drill, hand-putting so the ball just drops into the hole. When you successfully hand-putt the ball into the hole, select a new hole.

To Decrease Difficulty

- Hand-putt from a distance of 5 feet (1.5 meters) or less.
- Hand-putt on a flat surface, concentrating only on the pace of the putt.

To Increase Difficulty

- Use a hole with a large amount of break between you and the ball.
- Select a hole that has both a right-to-left break and left-to-right break as the ball approaches the hole.
- Use a putter instead of your hand.
- Set up croquet hoops on the putting green and play croquet using a golf ball and a putter.

Success Check

- Putt with sufficient pace so that the ball either drops into the hole or stops within 3 feet of the hole.
- You should be able to see which direction the ball breaks as it approaches the hole.

Score Your Success

Based on the second part of the drill, give yourself 1 point if the ball stops within 2 feet of the hole and 3 points if the ball is holed.

Your score ___

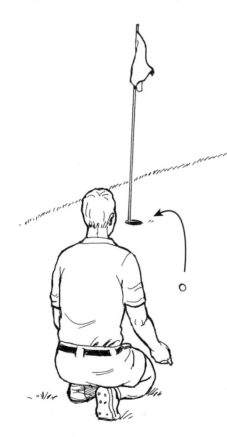

Figure 1.9 Hand-putting.

Strategic Putting Drill 2. *Strategic Putting on a Minicourse*

Set up a minicourse of six holes on the practice green. Each hole should be at least 6 feet from the previous hole. Hand-putt to each hole in order from hole 1 to hole 6. Play the course a second time and attempt to lower your score.

Success Check

- Putt with sufficient pace so that the ball either drops into the hole or stops within 3 feet of the hole.
- You should be able to see which direction the ball breaks as it approaches the hole.

Score Your Success

Three-putt hole = 1 point

Two-putt hole = 3 points

One-putt hole = 5 points

Your score ___

PUTTING SUCCESS SUMMARY

Success as a golfer is directly dependent on your skill as a putter. A long drive or an accurate iron shot can help you play well, but it is only when you master the ability to put the ball in the hole that you will get low scores. Putting skill can often compensate for a lack of skill in other areas of the game, but no skill can compensate for poor putting.

The good news is that putting is the easiest stroke to learn, practice, and master. Virtually anyone can become a good putter if they understand a few fundamental principles and spend time practicing. Putting is the great equalizer in golf. Developing a technically sound stroke,

practicing distance control, and studying how greens affect the roll of the ball are the three keys to successful putting. Learn the information and practice the drills in this step, and you will be well on your way to becoming a successful putter and golfer.

In the following list, record your point totals from each of the drills in this step and add them together. If you scored at least 180 out of 236 points, you're ready for the next step. If you scored fewer than 180 points, review the drills that gave you the most trouble before moving on to the next step.

Putting Stroke Drills

1.	Preshot Routine	___ out of 20
2.	Pendulum Progression	___ out of 20
3.	Target Line	___ out of 20
4.	Two Clubs	___ out of 30
5.	Distance Control	___ out of 20
6.	Par-2 Golf Course	___ out of 20
7.	Ladder Drill	___ out of 10
8.	Geometry Drills	___ out of 36

Strategic Putting Drills

1.	Hand-Putting	___ out of 30
2.	Strategic Putting on a Minicourse	___ out of 30
Total		**___ out of 236**

Now that you have developed your skill as a putter, you need to get the ball onto the green where your putting prowess can help you score low. While the putting stroke has many elements in common with shots hit with the other clubs, there are some basic differences. In the next step, we will look to master the fundamentals of a sound setup. These fundamentals apply to short shots near the green as well as long drives that get the ball off the tee and into play. A good setup for a reliable, repeatable golf swing is the next step you need to take.

Escrow No:3101716   **LOAN CONDITIONS/REQUIREMENTS**   Date: 12/21/92
Order No: 3101716   (EXHIBIT A)   Loan No: 79340394

VERIFICATION OF FOLLOWING OBLIGATION(S) PAID IN FULL

TO: WEYERHAUSER   FOR: $ 34,543.00
TO: ADVN MTG   FOR: $ 13,593.00
TO: FOR: $
TO: FOR: $
TO: FOR: $
TO: FOR: $
TO: FOR: $
TO: FOR: $
TO: FOR: $
TO: FOR: $

92 ?

97 - Mail

126 ?

631

Setting Up for the Shot

A successful golfer approaches each shot with deliberate, methodical efficiency. We often attribute great golf shots to powerful, rhythmic swings, but great golf shots are as much a result of the setup as they are the swing. In fact, a successful swing is usually impossible without a sound setup.

The good news is that it is relatively easy to master a sound setup. The setup provides the foundation on which to build a successful swing. Too often, however, golfers dismiss the setup and practice only full swings. These are the frustrated players you see spraying the ball around a golf course or practice range. If you want to be a successful golfer, give your setup the attention it deserves.

In this step, we take you through the keys to a successful setup for shots with wedges, irons, and metal clubs. Specifically, we will guide you through the principles of a proper grip, alignment, and setup. These principles apply to almost all full and partial golf swings. Many problems in golf are easily traceable to grip, alignment, or setup, so master these skills and you will be on your way to success.

GRIP KEYS AND STYLES

While there are different styles of grips, they all have four key elements. After explaining the four elements, we will discuss three common grip styles.

The first key to a good grip is to have the palms turned toward each other and the hands square to the target line (figure 2.1a). When the palms are turned toward each other, the hands work in unison, and when the hands are square to the target line, they bring the clubhead back to the ball, aiming directly at the target. Place your hands on the grip end of the club, palms turned toward each other, hands square to the target line. Looking down at your hands, two knuckles from your target-side hand should be visible and the Vs formed by your thumbs and forefingers should be pointing between your nontarget-side ear and shoulder.

The second key element is to grip the club in the fingers (figure 2.1b). Begin by gripping the club with the top, target-side hand. If you are right-handed, this will be your left hand. The grip of the club should rest in your fingers and press diagonally across your palm. The butt end of the club should rest under the fleshy part of the palm. The left thumb points down the right center of the club shaft (right-handed golfer).

Misstep

It is difficult to release the clubhead at contact.

Correction

You are holding the club in the palms of the hands rather than the fingers. Hold the club in the fingers between the first and second knuckles.

The third key to a good grip is to grip the club with the middle two fingers of the nontarget-side hand, palm turned toward the target line (figure 2.1c). After the target-side hand is holding the club, bring the other hand under the club so that the middle two fingers come to rest against the club grip. Close the fingers lightly around the club with the palm of the right hand (right-handed golfer) facing the target line. The thumb rests on the target side of the club, not on top.

The final key element is to bring your hands together by closing the fleshy part of the lower hand over the thumb of the upper hand. The Vs formed by the thumb and forefinger of each hand should be angled somewhere between the right shoulder and the right ear. Two knuckles from the target-side hand and one knuckle from the nontarget-side hand should be visible (figure 2.1d), allowing the club to return to this position on the downswing with the clubface square to the target. Grip pressure should be as light as possible; you should be able to hold on to the club, but your wrists should hinge naturally and easily.

Figure 2.1 Gripping the Club

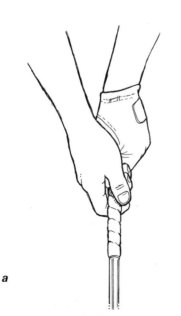

a

FIRST KEY:
HANDS ON GRIP

1. Turn the palms toward each other
2. Hands should be square to the target line

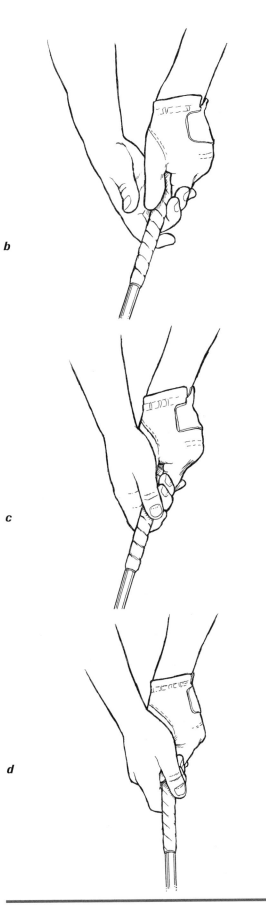

b

c

d

SECOND KEY: TARGET-SIDE HAND

1. Two knuckles of the target-side hand should be visible
2. Thumb and index finger of the target-side hand should be touching
3. V should be to the side of the rear ear
4. Club should rest diagonally across the fingers and palm
5. Butt of club should rest under the fleshy part of the palm
6. Hold the club more in the fingers than in the palm

THIRD KEY: NONTARGET-SIDE HAND

1. One knuckle of the nontarget-side hand should be visible
2. Thumb and index finger of the nontarget-side hand should be touching
3. Turn the palm toward the target
4. Hold the club in the fingers
5. Thumb should rest to the side of the club, not on top

FOURTH KEY: BOTH HANDS

1. Vs formed by the index finger and thumb should point at or slightly past the nontarget-side ear
2. Two knuckles of the target-side hand should be visible
3. Two knuckles of the nontarget-side hand should be visible
4. Fleshy part of the nontarget-side hand should completely cover the thumb of the target-side hand
5. Use light grip pressure

Misstep

The grip is turned so that the Vs formed by the index fingers and thumbs point outside the rear shoulder or directly at the chest.

Correction

Position the hands so that the Vs point just to the rear side of the ear on the nontarget-side of the body.

The Vs of your hands are a visible checkpoint. If the Vs point to your nontarget-side ear or shoulder, the hands are positioned to return the clubhead squarely to the golf ball. If the Vs point toward your nose or past your nontarget-side shoulder, the clubface will not return squarely to the ball. Use the Vs to ensure that your hands are properly positioned on the club.

Now that we've discussed the key elements of the grip, it's time to move on to grip styles. There are three popular styles for gripping a golf club: the overlap grip, interlock grip, and 10-finger or baseball grip. Try each style to discover which is the most comfortable and most effective for you.

The overlap grip is currently the most popular style. In the overlap grip, the smallest finger of the right hand rests on top and between the forefinger and middle finger of the left hand (figure 2.2a). This grip is used by Arnold Palmer, Jesper Parnevik, and Tiger Woods. Players with average or large hands generally find this grip the most comfortable.

The interlock grip is a slight variation of the overlap grip. In the interlock grip, the smallest finger of the right hand links or hooks with the forefinger of the right hand (figure 2.2b). This grip was made popular by Jack Nicklaus, but it is also used by many other touring professionals. Players with smaller hands and shorter fingers generally find this grip more comfortable.

Unlike the overlap and interlock grips, in the 10-finger or two-handed grip each hand directly and completely contacts the golf club. The fingers of both hands are placed on the golf club (figure 2.2c). This grip works well for women and senior players who may lack strength in their hands, but it is also used by professional golfers such as Bob Rosburg and Beth Daniel.

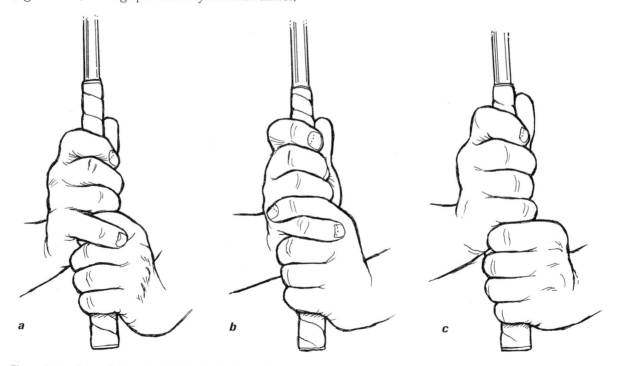

Figure 2.2   Grips: *(a)* overlap; *(b)* interlock; *(c)* 10-finger or baseball.

Misstep

You grip the club too tightly.

Correction

Imagine the club is a tube of toothpaste with the cap off and the top turned toward you. Hold the club firmly enough to swing it, but not so tightly that you squeeze toothpaste out as you swing.

Grip Drill 1. *Get a Grip*

Rest a golf club with the head on the ground and the grip leaning against your thigh. Grip the club first with your top hand (target-side hand) and then your lower hand. Raise the club so that your arms are straight out in front of you and the club points up (figure 2.3). Return the club to the ground and take a swing without using a ball.

Figure 2.3 Get a grip drill.

Practice the overlapping grip, the interlocking grip, and the baseball grip. Repeat until you have practiced all three grips five times each.

To Decrease Difficulty

- Focus on only one grip at a time. It is easiest to begin with the baseball grip.

To Increase Difficulty

- Repeat the drill with your eyes closed. Concentrate on feeling the proper grip and pressure.
- After you have raised the club and checked your grip, finish the drill by bringing the club back to the ground and taking a full swing at a ball.

Success Check

- Turn your palms toward each other.
- Grip the club primarily with the fingers, not the palms.
- Vs formed by the thumbs and index fingers of both hands should point just past your right ear (right-handed golfer).

Score Your Success

Have a partner evaluate your performance. Give yourself 1 point for every grip that includes the four key elements.

Your score ___

21

Grip Drill 2. *Random Grip*

Have a partner call out a grip style (overlap, interlocking, or baseball). Grip the club using that style. Repeat until your partner has called out each style five times.

Success Check

- Turn your palms toward each other.
- Grip the club primarily with the fingers, not the palms.

- Vs formed by the thumbs and index fingers of both hands should point just past your right ear (right-handed golfer).

Score Your Success

Correct grip = 1 point

Your score ____

Grip Drill 3. *Feeling the Pressure*

Grip a club using one of the three grips, whichever one feels comfortable. Hold the club upright, perpendicular to the ground. Relax your grip until you feel as if the club is about to slip out of your hands and fall to the ground; this is the proper pressure. Now turn the club down to the ground and take a full swing without a golf ball. Your grip pressure should not change at any time during your swing. Repeat 10 times.

Success Check

- Turn your palms toward each other.
- Grip the club primarily with the fingers, not the palms.
- Vs formed by the thumbs and index fingers of both hands should point just past your right ear (right-handed golfer).

Score Your Success

Full swing executed without increasing grip pressure = 1 point

Your score ____

SETUP TECHNIQUE

The setup is the stance a golfer takes in preparation for stroking the ball. The setup is also referred to as the address or posture. Body position in relation to the ball has a significant effect on the shape, direction, and distance of the golf shot. A proper setup allows you to generate a powerful, efficient, and accurate stroke. Taking the time to understand and practice the setup is critical to developing a successful golf swing.

Begin the setup a few yards behind the golf ball, facing your target (figure 2.4a). Identify the target, or where you want the ball to land, and imagine a line coming from the target back to the ball. If possible, imagine the ball in flight to the target. Once you can see the target line, pick out an intermediate target on the line, such as an oddly-shaped blade of grass, an old divot, or a twig, that is a foot or two in front of the ball but directly between you and the target. When you approach the ball and take your stance, it is much easier to align your club with an intermediate target than one that is several hundred yards away. Jack Nicklaus uses an intermediate target on every shot to aim the clubhead and align his body for the shot. Using an intermediate target will help your aim and alignment too.

Misstep

The ball consistently goes left or right of the target line.

Correction

Position a club on the ground parallel with your target line and in front of your feet. This will make it easier for you to align your thighs, hips, and shoulders to the target line.

Move to the ball and place your club behind the ball and in line with the intermediate target. Align your shoulders, hips, and thighs so they are parallel with this target line (figure 2.4b). It is virtually impossible to hit straight shots if the body is not aligned, so you must practice taking a stance with your body parallel with the target line. The alignment drill will help you develop this part of your setup (see page 26).

To complete the setup, bend forward from your hips or the tops of your thighs as if you are about to sit on a high stool (figure 2.4c). Your knees should bend slightly and your arms should hang directly under the shoulders. Your back must be straight to allow the club to swing freely under your shoulders, and your chin should be up so that your shoulders can move back easily on the backswing. Your weight should be evenly distributed between your feet.

Misstep

Your weight is on the heels, making it difficult to maintain your balance.

Correction

Move your weight to the center and slightly to the insides of both feet.

If you are setting up with a metal club, the ball should be in line with the left heel. If you are setting up for an iron shot, the ball should be just to the target side of the middle of your stance. The difference in location is due to the length of the club shafts: The shorter the shaft length, the closer to the middle of your stance the ball should be.

Misstep

The ball is positioned too far forward, causing you to pull the ball to the left.

Correction

Practice setting up with an iron by placing a club on the ground between your feet. This makes it easy to identify the ball position at address.

Figure 2.4 | Setting Up for Success

SET TARGET LINE

1. From behind the ball, select a target
2. Identify an intermediate target
3. Visualize the shot

SET BODY TO BALL POSITION

1. Move to the ball
2. Place the clubhead behind the ball and in line with the intermediate target
3. When using a metal club, be sure the ball is in front of the left heel
4. When using an iron, be sure the ball is slightly to the target side of the center of the stance

SET UP FOR SHOT

1. Position the feet shoulder-width apart
2. Evenly distribute your weight over both feet
3. Align the thighs, hips, and shoulders parallel with the target line
4. Bend forward from the hips, keeping your back straight and your chin up
5. Position the target-side shoulder slightly higher than the nontarget-side shoulder
6. Let your arms hang comfortably and directly under the shoulders

Misstep

You bend from the waist rather than the hips, making it difficult to maintain a straight back.

Correction

Check yourself in a mirror to ensure that your back is straight and not curved when in setup position.

As you will discover in the coming steps, at times you will want to modify the setup. When your feet, thighs, hips, and shoulders are aligned directly parallel with the target line, you are in a normal stance (see figure 2.4c). If you pull your target-side foot back from the target line and align the rest of your body with your feet, you are in an open stance (figure 2.5a) because your body is open to the target. The open stance is common for pitch shots, bunker shots, and fade shots. If you move your target-side foot closer to the target line and realign your body along this line, you are in a closed stance (figure 2.5b) because your body is closed to the target. The closed stance is common for hitting a draw.

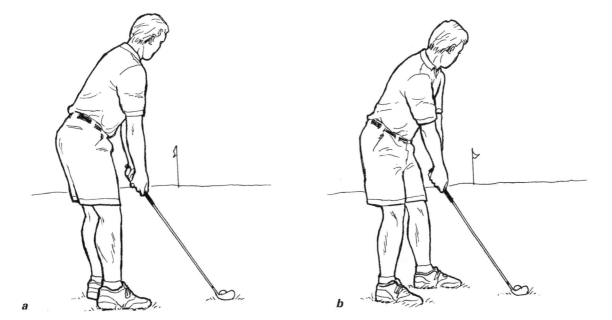

Figure 2.5 Stance variations: *(a)* open stance; *(b)* closed stance.

Setup Drill 1. *Intermediate Target*

From behind a ball, pick out a target, a target line, and an intermediate target. Approach the golf ball and take your address position. Have a partner place a golf club over your intermediate target and the clubface of your golf club. Repeat five times.

To Decrease Difficulty

- Place one tee in the ground 2 feet in front of your golf ball and one tee 2 feet behind your golf ball. When you take your address position, use the tees to help you align your golf club with the target line.

To Increase Difficulty

- Use a different target, target line, and intermediate target each time.

Success Check

- Shoulders, hips, and knees should be parallel with the intended target line.

Score Your Success

Clubface and intermediate target point directly at the target = 1 point

Your score ___

Setup Drill 2. *Alignment Drill*

With a club and a ball, pick out a target and target line and take your address position. Have a partner check your alignment by placing the shaft of a club against your shoulders, hips, and knees to make sure they are parallel with your intended target line (figure 2.6). Repeat five times.

To Decrease Difficulty

- Place a club behind the golf ball with the handle of the club pointing toward the target. When you take your address position, use the golf club to help you identify your target line.

To Increase Difficulty

- From behind the ball, pick out a target and an intermediate target, then move to the ball and take your setup. Repeat five times using five different targets.

Success Check

- Shoulders, hips, and knees should be parallel with the intended target line.

Score Your Success

Shoulders, hips, and knees parallel with the target line = 1 point

Your score ___

Figure 2.6   Alignment drill.

Setup Drill 3. **Parallel Clubs**

Place two clubs parallel on the ground along the target line, one club at the top of the ball, one along your feet (figure 2.7). Address and then stroke the ball. Repeat 10 times.

Figure 2.7 Parallel clubs drill.

To Decrease Difficulty

- Execute the shot using a pitching wedge or 9-iron.

To Increase Difficulty

- Use five different clubs to execute the shot. Use each club twice before changing clubs. Start with a higher-lofted club and progress to a lower-lofted club.

Success Check

- Visualize each shot from behind the ball.
- As you step to the ball, place the clubhead square to the intermediate target.

Score Your Success

Shot starts along the target line and moves toward the target = 2 points

Your score ___

Setup Drill 4. *Partner Evaluation*

Approach a golf ball from behind and take the proper setup, concentrating on the points covered in figure 2.4 (page 24). Have a partner check that you are set to the target line, your body is properly positioned to the ball, and your body posture is set up for the shot. Repeat 5 times.

To Decrease Difficulty

- Assume your setup without a ball or golf club.

To Increase Difficulty

- Change clubs with each setup.
- Pick a different target line each time you take your setup.

Success Check

- Your setup should meet all the points covered in figure 2.4 (page 24).

Score Your Success

Place the clubhead behind the ball and in line with the intermediate target = 1 point

For a metal club, the ball is in front of the left heel; for an iron, the ball is slightly to the target side = 1 point

Feet are shoulder-width apart = 1 point

Weight is evenly distributed over both feet = 1 point

Thighs, hips, and shoulders are parallel with the target line = 1 point

Forward bend is forward from the hips and your back is straight and your chin is up = 1 point

Target-side shoulder is slightly higher than the nontarget-side shoulder = 1 point

Arms hang comfortably and directly under shoulders = 1 point

Your score ___

SETUP STRATEGY

When you stand behind the ball to select a target, you will need to make two strategic decisions. First, the target you choose will influence which club you use. For example, if you are facing the second shot on a par-5 hole, will you attempt to reach the green or will you lay up to a closer but safer target? In general, it is better to take the more conservative approach since penalty strokes from lost balls, balls hit into water, or poor lies add many more strokes than an extra stroke from playing to a closer target. Regardless of the club, club selection only influences ball position in the setup. With shorter-shafted irons, the ball is played closer to the center of the stance. Longer metal clubs require you to move the ball more in line with your left heel. Club selection is explained in greater depth in step 9.

The second strategic decision involves what shape the shot will take. Do you want the shot to go left to right (a fade for a right-handed golfer and a draw for a left-hander), right to left (a draw for a right-handed golfer and a fade for a left-hander), or straight? For a beginner who sometimes struggles just to get the ball airborne, the idea of stroking a ball so that it moves in a predictable path seems daunting, but getting the ball to fade or draw is not all that difficult because this path is determined primarily by the setup. Executing these shots requires minor adjustments to the grip and the stance, in addition to a great deal of practice. Shaping a golf shot is an advanced skill, and you will need a lot of practice before you can shape a shot on the golf course.

If the ball is to go straight, the Vs formed by the index fingers and thumbs should point toward the nontarget-side ear. In the stance for a straight shot, shoulders, hips, and knees all should be parallel with a line running directly toward the target.

In a fade shot, the ball moves in flight from left to right (right-handed golfer). This shot is useful for directing a ball over or around a hazard. For example, if a water hazard lines a fairway on the right, you might want to start the tee shot on the left side of the fairway with a small amount of fade so that it moves back to the middle of the fairway in flight. If you slightly mishit the shot and it goes straight, you will still be in the fairway and far from the hazard. To execute this shot, move the Vs until they point closer to your nose. Open your stance by moving your knees, hips, and shoulders so that they align to the left of where you want the ball to land. A fade won't travel as far as a straight shot, so consider using a club with a little less loft than usual for the distance you need the shot to travel.

The opposite of a fade is a draw. For a right-handed golfer, a draw moves the ball from right to left. Like the fade, a draw is useful for maneuvering a ball around hazards and natural objects on the course. To execute a draw, move the Vs so that they point just past the nontarget-side shoulder, making sure you move the hands rather than the club to achieve the desired results. Next, close your stance by aligning your knees, hips, and shoulders to the right of the intended landing area. A draw will travel farther than a straight shot, so consider using a club with slightly more loft than usual.

Setup Strategy Drill 1. *Ball Position*

You will need four clubs for this drill: a pitching wedge, 6-iron, driver, and 3-iron. The shorter the shaft, the more the ball is played in the middle of the stance. Place a golf ball on the practice range and lay the 3-iron so that the clubhead points toward the golf ball and the grip end points toward the spot at which you will address the ball. The shaft should be perpendicular to the target line.

Begin the drill behind the ball. Pick out a target and go through your normal setup routine. The only change is the position of the ball in your stance, which is determined by the club you are using. First, set up using a pitching wedge, positioning the golf ball so that it is aligned in the middle of the stance between both feet. Second, set up using the 6-iron. The ball should be approximately 2 inches (5 centimeters) closer to the target than the middle of the stance. Third, set up with the driver and the ball on a tee. The ball should be in line with the heel of your target-side foot. Each time you set up, use the 3-iron on the ground to check for proper ball position. Repeat five times with each club.

Success Check

- With the pitching wedge, the ball should be in the middle of stance.
- With the 6-iron, the ball should be approximately 2 inches closer to the target than the middle of the stance.
- With the driver, the ball should be in line with the target-side heel.

Score Your Success

Correct setup with pitching wedge = 1 point each time

Correct setup with 6-iron = 1 point each time

Correct setup with driver = 1 point each time

Your score ___

Setup Strategy Drill 2. *Straights, Fades, and Draws*

Use a 3-metal or 5-metal. To gain maximum benefits from this drill, place the ball on the tee. Hit a straight shot, then a fade, then a draw, each time making the appropriate adjustment in grip and stance. Repeat the cycle of three shots 10 times. Be patient—this skill takes time to develop.

To Decrease Difficulty

- Take half swings, bringing the club only halfway back and swinging it halfway through. This provides more control, making the shots easier to hit. The ball will not fly as far in the air, but the shape of the shot—straight, fade, or draw—will let you know if your setup was correct. Once you are comfortable shaping the shot, return to the full swing.

To Increase Difficulty

- Alternate between a 3-metal and a 7-iron after each three-shot cycle.
- Hit all shots to the same target.

Success Check

- For a straight shot, Vs should point between the nontarget ear and shoulder, and knees, hips, and shoulders should be parallel with the target line.
- For a fade, Vs should point toward the nose and the stance should be open to the target (right-handed golfer would appear to be aimed left of the target).

- For a draw, Vs should point past the non-target shoulder and the stance should be closed to the target (right-handed golfer would appear to be aimed right of the target).

Score Your Success

Correct stance and grip on straight shot = 1 point each shot

Straight shot goes straight = 1 point each shot

Correct stance and grip on fade shot = 1 point each shot

Fade shot moves left to right (right-handed golfer) = 1 point each shot

Correct stance and grip on draw shot = 1 point each shot

Draw shot moves right to left (right-handed golfer) = 1 point each shot

Your score ____

Setup Strategy Drill 3. *Called Shots*

Niclas Fasth likes to finish a long day of practice by hitting a variety of golf shots simply for the joy of hitting the ball. At the 2003 World Championships at Kiawah Island, the sun was setting but Niclas was still on the practice range. To provide a bit of a challenge, others called out shots for him to hit—straight, fade, or draw. To increase the challenge, they called out the shot just as he reached the top of his backswing.

Find a partner. One of you takes 10 swings as the other calls out the shot (straight, fade, or draw). Call out the shot when your partner is addressing the ball so that she can make the grip and stance adjustment before starting the swing.

To Decrease Difficulty

- Have your partner call the shot before you take your stance.
- Execute the shot using a pitching wedge or 9-iron.

To Increase Difficulty

- Have your partner call the shot just as you begin to take the club away.
- Increase the amount the ball turns as it fades or draws by altering your grip and stance.

Success Check

- For a right-handed player hitting a draw shot, the Vs of the thumb and forefinger should point past the left shoulder and the stance should be closed (facing to the left of the intended target).
- For a right-handed player hitting a fade shot, the Vs of the thumb and forefinger should point toward the nose and the stance should be open (facing to the right of the intended target).

Score Your Success

Called shot is successfully executed = 2 points

Your score ____

SETUP SUCCESS SUMMARY

Grip and setup are two of the most critical aspects of successful golf. Without a good grip and setup, it will not be possible to gain low scores on the course. It is therefore vital to carefully study the information in this step and undertake the practice activities in earnest. Those who convince themselves that this information is not important are destined to remain novices for a long and frustrating time.

The grip and setup require constant vigilance. Fortunately, you can practice them anywhere. Keep a golf club handy and periodically practice taking the grip, checking your technique. You can also check and practice the setup with or without a ball or even with or without a club.

When checking the setup, particularly your posture, a mirror can be helpful. Revisit these areas of your game often, and when a problem occurs in your swing, check grip and setup first, as many problems in a golf swing can be traced to these two factors. The good news is that these areas often are the easiest to practice and correct.

Record your point totals from each of the drills in this step and add them together. If you scored at least 150 out of 205 points, you're ready for the next step. If you scored fewer than 150 points, review the drills that gave you the most trouble before you move on to the next step.

Grip Drills

1. Get a Grip   ___ out of 15

2. Random Grip   ___ out of 15

3. Feeling the Pressure   ___ out of 10

Setup Drills

1. Intermediate Target   ___ out of 5

2. Alignment Drill   ___ out of 5

3. Parallel Clubs   ___ out of 20

4. Partner Evaluation   ___ out of 40

Setup Strategy Drills

1. Ball Position   ___ out of 15

2. Straights, Fades, and Draws   ___ out of 60

3. Called Shots   ___ out of 20

Total   ___ *out of 205*

In this step, you have learned that to have a good golf stroke, you need to have a good grip and setup. These are the foundation upon which a golf game is built. In *Getting Back to Basics* (1992), Tom Watson, a five-time British Open champion, wrote, "I can almost always predict when my 15-handicap friends are going to hit a good shot, because they will be set up well" (page 28).

Now that you understand and have practiced these fundamentals, you are ready to apply them to a golf shot. In keeping with the philosophy that golf is best learned from the hole back to the tee, the next step introduces you to the chip. The chip shot gets a ball that is just off the green onto the green and close to, if not in, the hole. If you can chip and putt, you can play with anyone, because you can score. You already know about putting, so take what you learned in this step and move to the next: Chipping to the Green.

Chipping to the Green

Despite a golfer's best effort, an approach shot often misses the green. At times you will find yourself just a few feet from the green with high grass or some other obstacle between the ball and the putting green. The shot called for at this moment is a chip shot.

A chip shot is a low-trajectory shot intended to land on the green and roll to the hole. The best golfers are proficient at chipping the ball directly into the hole, but that comes with hours and hours of practice.

To produce a low-trajectory shot that has sufficient roll, an iron club rather than a wedge is used. Most often golfers use a 7-, 8-, or 9-iron to make a chip shot, but with the proper technique just about any club will work. An iron with lower loft creates a lower ball trajectory and therefore gets the ball to land on the green more quickly and produces more roll toward the hole. For example, if you hit a chip shot with a 7-iron, the ball will land more quickly and produce more roll than the same stroke made with a 9-iron. You will need to practice chipping with different irons to learn the ball flight and roll characteristics you can achieve with each club.

CHIP SHOTS

As with any golf shot, preparation helps ensure solid ball contact and the desired flight pattern. The setup for a successful chip shot contains three adjustments:

1. Ball is back in the stance.
2. Hands are forward of the ball.
3. Weight is more on the target side of the body.

These three adjustments work together to give the clubhead a slightly descending angle, resulting in the crisp contact necessary for a controllable chip shot. Because the chip shot requires a short swing with little force, the feet are closer together than on a full swing and the target-side foot is turned out a bit more (figure 3.1a).

The key to a successful chip shot is accuracy. Follow the setup procedure that you learned in step 2. Start behind the ball, pick out a target (landing area), visualize the line you want the ball to roll along, and pick out an intermediate target. Move up to the ball, place your club behind the ball, and square it to your intermediate target. Then make the three adjustments to the setup. First, place about 80 percent of your

33

weight on your target-side foot and keep it there throughout the swing. Second, position the ball back in the stance, directly in front of the big toe of your nontarget-side foot. Third, grip down on the handle so that you almost touch the shaft and position the grip of the club in front of your target-side thigh. These three adjustments will help you make clean, solid contact with the golf ball and produce a predictable flight.

Because the ball does not need to travel a great distance, the shoulders provide all the power for the chip shot. Setting the lower body by bending the knees and maintaining that position throughout the swing makes the chip shot easier to execute. In the chip shot, the lower body is used only for balance; too much lower-body action makes it difficult to contact the ball squarely. Once you set your feet, legs, and hips, they should move little throughout the swing.

Once the body is set in the proper address for the chip shot, the next phase is the stroke (figure 3.1b). Think of the stroke as a rocking motion of the shoulders, much like a putt. Initiate the backswing by turning your shoulders away from the target. Initiate the downswing by returning the shoulders back to and through their original position. The arms and shoulders form a triangle, with the hands and club representing the apex of the triangle. Because the shoulders provide most of the movement, the triangle is maintained throughout the swing. To promote a steeper angle back to the ball and achieve a crisper shot, the wrists hinge slightly up on the takeaway. The length of the shot determines the length of the backswing. The farther the ball must travel, the longer the backswing must be.

Misstep

You hit on top of the ball, resulting in no loft.

Correction

This error is normally caused by flipping the wrists. If the wrists bend, the sole of the club strikes the ball rather than the clubface. Keep your wrists firm and practice the address drill (page 36).

Misstep

You hit behind the ball, striking the ground first and losing distance on the shot.

Correction

If your weight is on the wrong foot at the point of contact, you will hit behind the ball. At address, shift approximately 75 percent of your weight to the target side of your body.

The chip shot is a single, smooth motion. The club travels back from the ball and then returns to and through the ball with the golfer in a balanced position. Because the weight is loaded to the target side during the address, there is little lower-body movement. The primary chipping motion is made with the shoulders and the hands and arms naturally follow the shoulders.

Allow the club to follow through about the same distance as the club traveled on the backswing (figure 3.1c). In the follow-through, body weight is primarily on the target-side foot, the left wrist (right-handed player) remains straight, the hips and shoulders angle toward the target, the clubface points directly on the line the ball just traveled, and the body is balanced.

Misstep

The ball goes too far or stops short of the hole.

Correction

Try checking the loft of the club. A lower loft results in a lower trajectory and more run to the ball, while a higher loft results in a higher trajectory, softer landing, and less run. Practice the club selection drill (page 40). Also make sure the length of the backswing and forward swing are the same. Practice the ladder drill (page 10).

Figure 3.1 Executing the Chip Shot

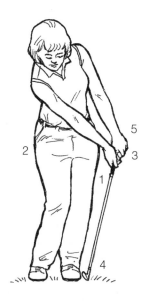

a   b   c

PREPARATION

1. Grip down on the club close to the shaft
2. Position the hands ahead of the ball
3. Flex the knees
4. Make sure the ball is positioned off the right ankle
5. Make sure your weight favors the target side of the body
6. Use the straightest-faced club that will carry the ball 3 to 6 feet onto the green and allow it to roll to the hole

EXECUTION

1. Follow your preshot routine (same as for putting)
2. Keep the hands ahead of the clubhead all the way through the stroke
3. Use a pendulum action back and through the ball
4. Keep the backswing and downswing approximately the same length
5. Keep the head and lower body still for better control

FOLLOW-THROUGH

1. Finish with your weight on the target side of the body
2. Hips face the target
3. Keep the forward swing the same length as the backswing
4. Clubface is square to the target line
5. Keep the target-side wrist straight

Misstep

The ball consistently goes offline to the left or right.

Correction

Be sure your knees, hips, and shoulders are parallel with the intended target line. Practice the parallel clubs drill (page 27) and the alignment drill (page 26) with a partner.

Chip Shot Drill 1. *Address Drill*

Set a ball 3 to 5 feet from a putting green. Approach the ball and get in the address position for a chip shot. Check the three key factors for a proper setup. Repeat the drill five times each with a 5-iron, 7-iron, and 9-iron. Give yourself 1 point each time you use proper ball position, your hands are ahead of the clubhead, and most of your weight is on your target-side foot.

Next, take the proper setup to a ball. Practice the chipping motion, emphasizing keeping the target-side wrist straight. The left hand leads and pulls the club through the contact zone. You should feel as if you are pulling the starting cord of a lawn mower with your left hand. Your left wrist should be straight, not bent, after each shot. Repeat 10 times.

Hit 10 chip shots to three different holes with an 8-iron. Check for proper address with each chip. Have a partner observe that the ball position is correct, your hands are ahead of the ball, and your weight is on the target side of the body. Give yourself 2 points for every chip you finish with your hands ahead of the clubhead.

To Decrease Difficulty

- Set up without a ball. Execute chip shots, emphasizing the shoulder turn with minimal arm and hand movement. The clubface should just brush the grass.

To Increase Difficulty

- Repeat the first two parts of the drill with the ball on an upward slope to the green.
- Repeat the first two parts of the drill with the ball on a downward slope to the green.

Success Check

- Weight should be primarily on the target-side foot.
- Keep your hands ahead of the clubhead at all times.
- Grip down on the club.

Score Your Success

0 to 14 points = 2 points
15 to 19 points = 3 points
20 to 24 points = 6 points
25 to 29 points = 8 points
30 to 35 points = 10 points
Your score ___

Chip Shot Drill 2. *Pyramid*

This drill develops distance control. Use a 7-iron to chip a ball approximately 10 feet onto a practice green. Chip the next ball so that it stops 3 to 5 feet past the first ball and 1 to 3 feet to the left. Repeat until you have chipped five balls. The last ball should stop approximately 30 feet directly in front of you. Then reverse the drill so that each ball comes to rest 3 to 5 feet short of the previous chip shot and 1 to 3 feet to the left. When you have completed the drill, the 10 chip shots should form a pyramid (figure 3.2).

To Decrease Difficulty

- Chip five balls so that each ball passes the previous chip.
- Chip five balls so that each ball stops closer to you than the previous chip.

To Increase Difficulty

- Attempt to make the pyramid apex no farther than 20 feet away.
- Use a different club for each distance.
- Perform the drill on an undulating portion of the practice green.

Success Check

- Perform the stroke with a pendulum-like action, using the shoulders.
- At the finish the hands and wrists should be firm and ahead of the clubhead.
- Maintain the spine angle throughout the stroke.

Score Your Success

More than two shots off = 0 points

Two shots off = 5 points

Perfect pyramid = 10 points

Your score ___

Chip Shot Drill 3. *Club Chips*

Place three clubs on a practice green at distances of 10, 20, and 30 feet. Place the clubs so that the shafts are square to you and completely visible (in other words, do not place two clubs in a direct line running from you). Chip a ball to the club closest to you, chip a second ball to the club 20 feet away, and chip a third ball to the club 30 feet away. Repeat 10 times for a total of 30 chip shots.

Success Check

- Perform the stroke with a pendulum-like action, using the shoulders.
- At the finish the hands and wrists should be firm and ahead of the clubhead.
- Maintain the spine angle throughout the stroke.

Score Your Success

Ball stops within 3 feet of the target club = 1 point each shot

Ball comes to rest against the target club = 2 points each shot

Your score ___

Chip Shot Drill 4. *Sink 'Em*

Chip a ball to a hole that is near the edge of the green and close to you, concentrating on sinking the ball into the cup. Repeat 10 times.

To Increase Difficulty

- Chip to a hole 20 to 30 feet away.
- Select three different holes and vary the target hole on each shot.
- Repeat the drill using three different irons (5, 7, and 9 or 6, 8, and putting wedge).
- Have a chipping contest with a partner. Whoever gets closest to the hole wins the hole. Take turns picking out the hole, and use the same club and the same ball.

Success Check

- Keep the hands ahead of the clubhead throughout the stroke.
- Keep the lower body set so it moves little throughout the stroke.

Score Your Success

Chip shot stops within 3 feet of the hole = 1 point

Holed chip shot = 3 points

Your score ___

Chip Shot Drill 5. *Hole It Out*

Putting the ball in the hole is known as holing it out. That is the purpose of this drill—to hole it out. Select three holes within 30 feet of the edge of the practice green, numbering the holes 1 to 3. Chip five balls to each hole for a total of 15 chip shots. Hit the first chip shot to hole 1, the second to hole 2, the third to hole 3, the fourth to hole 1, and so on.

To Decrease Difficulty

- Chip five balls to hole 1, then five balls to hole 2, and then five balls to hole 3. This will help you gain a better feel for distance.

To Increase Difficulty

- Select three holes that are a significant distance from each other. For example, hole 1 is close to you, hole 2 is approximately 30 feet away, and hole 3 is approximately 60 feet away.
- Use three different irons. Select the iron you think will get the ball closest to that particular hole.

Score Your Success

Chip shot stops within 3 feet of the target hole = 1 point

Holed chip shot = 3 points

Your score ___

Chip Shot Drill 6. *Up and Down*

Many golf instructors and touring pros consider this drill to be the most effective method for lowering scores. Chip a ball to a hole, take a putter, and continue putting until you hole the ball. Attempt to get the ball in the hole with one chip shot and one putt. Repeat 10 times with 10 different holes.

To Decrease Difficulty

- Complete the drill using only one hole that is within 6 feet of you.

To Increase Difficulty

- Vary the distance of the holes. The closest hole should be no farther than 10 feet and the farthest hole should be at least 60 feet.
- Select a different iron for each chip according to the distance you wish the ball to travel in the air and roll on the green.
- Select holes with different undulations— left-to-right break, right-to-left break, uphill, and downhill.

Success Check

- Maintain the triangle of shoulders, arms, and club throughout the shot.
- Slightly hinge the wrists on the takeaway for longer shots.
- Maintain balance.

Score Your Success

Three strokes to hole the ball (a chip and two putts) = 1 point

Two strokes to hole the ball (a chip and a putt) = 3 points

Holed chip shot = 5 points

Your score ___

Chip Shot Drill 7. *Chipping Course*

Select nine different holes on a practice green and number them 1 through 9. Chip and putt a ball into each hole in order. You may change clubs or use the same club for all nine holes. Each hole represents a par 3 (one shot to get on the green and two strokes to putt out). Count the total number of strokes needed to complete the nine holes.

Success Check

- Maintain the triangle of shoulders, arms, and club through the shot.
- Hinge the wrists slightly on the takeaway for longer shots.
- Maintain balance.

Score Your Success

29 strokes or more needed to complete the course = 5 points

24 to 28 strokes needed to complete the course = 10 points

18 to 23 strokes needed to complete the course = 15 points

17 strokes or fewer needed to complete the course = 20 points

Your score ___

CHIPPING STRATEGY

Like any shot in golf, the first step in making a chip shot is to determine what you want the ball to do and the second step is to figure out how to make that happen. You must visualize the chip shot, imagining the trajectory of the ball, where the ball will land on the green, and the path it will take toward the hole.

Because a successful chip shot has a low trajectory, lands quickly on the green, and rolls up to the hole, the first strategic decision is club selection. Club choice determines both the trajectory and the amount of roll. If you are 2 or 3 feet from the green, a low-lofted club such as a 4-, 5-, or 6-iron may be the best choice. If you are 10 to 15 feet from the green, an 8- or 9-iron or even a pitching wedge may be the best choice. Chip to different targets using different clubs to learn which clubs provide the ball flight and roll characteristics you need for the best chance of holing the chip shot.

A second strategic decision is determining the path the ball will take as it rolls on the green. This process is referred to as reading the green and was described in step 1 (see page 12). From this perspective, a chip shot and a putt have a great deal in common, as the intent of the shot is for the ball to roll into the hole. After visualizing the shot and choosing the club and ball path, the next step is to properly execute the shot.

Chipping Strategy Drill 1. *Club Selection*

Select a hole on the practice green within 30 feet of your golf ball. Experiment with different clubs to discover which club gets the ball consistently closer to the hole. Note changes in where the ball lands on the green and the path it takes as it rolls to the hole. Using a 6-, 7-, 8-, and 9-iron, hit at least three chip shots with each club.

To score the drill, hit a chip shot with 5-, 7-, and 9-irons to a single hole that is 10 to 15 feet away. Hit three shots with each club.

To Decrease Difficulty

- Chip the ball to a towel placed on the practice green rather than a golf hole.
- Select one club (6-, 7-, 8-, or 9-iron) and determine which hole on the practice green you can consistently chip closest to with that club.

To Increase Difficulty

- Chip to a hole that is uphill. Does this change your club selection?
- Chip to a hole that is downhill. Does this change your club selection?

Success Check

- Visualize the landing area and roll to the hole for each chip.
- Read the green to determine if you need more or less club loft to compensate for an uphill or downhill chip shot.

Score Your Success

Chip lands on the green = 1 point

Ball stops within 6 feet of the hole = 2 points

Holed chip shot = 3 points

Your score ___

Chipping Strategy Drill 2. *Modified Hazard*

A chip shot is often used to clear a hazard between the ball and the putting green, and this drill simulates such a situation. Place a golf bag approximately 10 yards (9 meters) in front of your ball. Chip over the bag to golf clubs placed on the green at 20, 30, and 40 feet (6, 9, and 12 meters) (figure 3.3). Experiment with clubs with different lofts and note their effect on the trajectory of your shot.

Now you are ready to score the drill. Place four golf clubs at 3, 6, 9, and 12 feet (1, 2, 3, and 4 meters) onto the green. Chip the first ball so that it lands between the first and second clubs, chip the second ball so that it lands between the second and third clubs, and chip the third ball so that it lands between the third and fourth clubs. Repeat five times for a total of 15 chip shots.

To Decrease Difficulty

- Repeat the drill with a pitching or sand wedge.

To Increase Difficulty

- Repeat the drill, setting clubs at 5, 10, and 15 feet from the edge of the green.
- Practice chipping over a bunker to a practice green.
- Repeat the drill, setting clubs at 50, 60, and 70 feet (15, 18, and 21 meters).

Success Check

- Visualize the trajectory and roll of the ball before to stroking each chip shot.
- Focus on where you want the ball to land, not the obstacle.

Score Your Success

Chip shot lands in the intended target area = 2 points

Your score ___

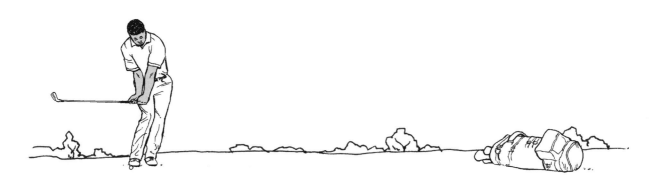

Figure 3.3 Modified hazard drill.

CHIPPING SUCCESS SUMMARY

All players eventually find themselves close to but not quite on the green. According to Bobby Jones the secret to low scores is turning three strokes into two. You can miss the green and still get the ball up to and into the hole in two shots (a chip and a putt) if you have an effective chip shot. If you become a very good chipper, you will occasionally chip your balls into the hole. The more proficient you become at chipping, the greater your success on the scorecard will be.

Like putting, chipping is not one of the most glamorous skills in golf, but it is critical to your success and therefore requires continued practice. Also like putting, because this shot is a short-distance shot favoring accuracy over power, it is easier to gain proficiency in. Use the drills in this chapter to increase your skill and the checklists to assess your progress. When you play, monitor your ups and downs because you will find that many strokes can be saved with a good chip shot.

Record your point totals from each of the drills in this step and add them together. If you scored at least 150 out of 282 points, you're ready for the next step. If you scored fewer than 150 points, review the drills that gave you the most trouble before moving on to the next step.

Chip Shot Drills

  1. Address Drill   ___ out of 10

  2. Pyramid   ___ out of 10

  3. Club Chips   ___ out of 60

  4. Sink 'Em   ___ out of 30

  5. Hole It Out   ___ out of 45

  6. Up and Down   ___ out of 50

  7. Chipping Course   ___ out of 20

Chipping Strategy Drills

  1. Club Selection   ___ out of 27

  2. Modified Hazard   ___ out of 30

Total   ___ *out of 282*

A chip shot is the best shot for getting a ball that is just off the green onto the green and rolling toward or into the hole. Practice this shot often and you will shoot lower scores.

At times you will find yourself too far from the green for an effective chip shot but not far enough for a full swing with a 9-iron. At other times, you may need the ball to land softly on the green and roll very little. Both of these situations call for a pitch shot, which is covered in the next step.

Pitching From Farther Away

A pitch shot is similar to a chip shot in that the ball flies through the air to reach the green and then rolls to the hole. However, a pitch shot is used when the ball must fly farther to reach the green, typically when the ball is 10 to 90 yards (9 to 82 meters) from the green. With its high trajectory and modest roll, the pitch shot gets the ball over bumps in the fairway, past the rough, over a green-side bunker, or even beyond a small pond and still allows the ball to sit when it lands and not roll off the green. Because the majority of shots in a round of golf are played from fewer than 100 yards, a player who becomes proficient at putting, chipping, and pitching—the skills of the short game—will make significant progress in shooting lower scores.

In contrast to the chip shot's low trajectory and significant roll, the pitch shot flies higher and rolls very little. To achieve a higher trajectory and less roll, the pitch shot requires a higher-lofted iron. Wedges, a special category of irons, are used for pitch shots. Common wedges include the pitching wedge (45 to 52 degrees of loft), sand wedge (52 to 58 degrees of loft), and lob wedge (58 to 64 degrees of loft). The higher the loft of the club, the higher the trajectory of the ball, the shorter distance the ball will fly, and the less distance the ball will roll when it lands.

PITCH SHOTS

A successful pitch shot requires accuracy and distance control, and proper setup is key to both. As with a chip shot, the pitch shot does not require a full, powerful swing, so begin the setup by identifying precisely where you would like the ball to land on the green. When selecting the landing target, remember that the ball will roll gently when it lands.

With the target firmly in mind, set up in a relatively narrow, balanced stance with the feet less than shoulder-width apart (figure 4.1a). To promote a smooth swing, open the stance a bit by pulling the target-side foot back a few inches and pointing the toes toward the target. Because pitching wedges have shorter shafts, play the ball in the middle of the stance to promote clean, crisp contact. Move the hands slightly ahead of the ball.

Once you are locked onto your target and have set up properly, you are ready to begin the swing (figure 4.1b). Turn the shoulders away from the target, letting the shoulders draw the club back.

The arms and hands will naturally follow the turn of the shoulders, as will the hips and legs. The backswing is the key to distance control: The shorter the backswing, the shorter the shot. With practice, you will learn how far the backswing needs to go for the ball to land on target.

Distance control and accuracy are possible only when you execute the pitch shot in a relaxed, rhythmic manner. A pitch shot uses the same smooth, easy motion as tossing a ball underhanded into a bucket. Begin the downswing (figure 4.1c) by shifting the weight from the back foot to the target side and letting the rest of the body follow. The club should feel like it is simply dropping back to the ball as the shoulders and chest unwind toward the target. The speed of the shot slowly accelerates through contact and a high finish. At impact, your left wrist is firm and straight, your focus is on stroking the ball firmly toward the target, and your hands are ahead of the clubhead. Don't rush the downswing.

In the follow-through, the club follows the ball toward the target for as long as possible (figure 4.1d). You should finish on balance with your body weight on the target-side foot, hips and chest facing the target, and hands above the shoulders. Before you lift your eyes to see your shot, focus on the location where the ball was before contact. In other words, resist the temptation to look up too soon because this may cause the shoulders to pull the club offline. Make sure the ball is well gone before you look for it.

If you have trouble hitting the ball with loft, check your wrist position. If you flip your wrists in an effort to lift the ball into the air, you may hit the top of the ball and not get any loft. Many players attempt to scoop the ball up using their wrists. When the left wrist bends, the sole of the club rather than the clubface strikes the ball, causing the dreaded skulled shot. Execute the shot by turning the shoulders and chest, letting the arms, hands, and club simply follow.

Misstep

You hit the top of the ball, resulting in no loft.

Correction

This error may be caused by a posture problem. Wedges are the shortest clubs in the bag and require greater knee and hip bend to properly hit down on the ball. Check your posture, particularly during the swing, as you may have the tendency to raise up as the club approaches the ball. Maintain proper posture from address to follow-through.

If you find you are hitting the ground before the club reaches the ball, you may be decelerating on the downswing. The pitch shot demands distance control, and a common error is to overswing on the backswing and then compensate by decelerating on the downswing. This results in the club hitting the ground before it reaches the ball. Shorten the backswing and be mildly aggressive on the downswing. You'll find it easier to make solid contact, which makes it easier to control the distance the ball travels.

Misstep

You hit behind the ball, striking the ground first and losing distance on the shot.

Correction

Because the pitch shot uses an abbreviated swing, it is common for players to leave their weight on their nontarget-side foot. Be sure to move your weight to the target-side foot before contacting the ball.

Figure 4.1 Executing the Pitch Shot

a

PREPARATION

1. Set up in a narrow, balanced stance
2. Position the feet less than shoulder-width apart
3. Pull the target-side foot back a few inches and point the toes toward the target
4. Play the ball in the middle of the stance
5. Position the hands slightly ahead of the ball

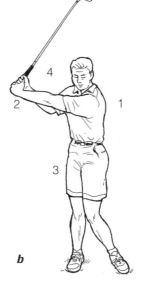

b

BACKSWING

1. Turn the shoulders away from the target to begin the swing
2. Allow the arms, hands, and club to naturally follow the turn of the shoulders
3. Allow the hips and legs to turn naturally in response to shoulder turn
4. Use the length of the backswing to determine flight distance

c

DOWNSWING

1. Begin the downswing by shifting weight from the back to the front foot
2. Drop the club back to the ball as the shoulders and chest unwind to the target
3. Build shot speed slowly to accelerate through the ball
4. At impact, keep the left wrist firm and square to the target
5. Execute the shot in a relaxed, rhythmic manner

d

FOLLOW-THROUGH

1. Let the club follow the ball toward the target
2. Finish with body weight on the target-side foot, elbows high
3. Focus on the spot where the ball was before contact and then lift your eyes to follow the ball

Misstep

The ball consistently goes off the target line.

Correction

Check your alignment. Be sure your knees, hips, and shoulders are all parallel with the intended target line. Try the string drill on this page.

Misstep

The ball goes too far or falls short.

Correction

Check your swing length. Evaluate the length of the backswing and forward swing on the pitch shot; they should be the same. Practice the ladder drill on page 10.

Pitch Shot Drill 1. *String Drill*

To hit crisp pitch shots, your weight must be forward and you must bring the club to the ball so that you contact the ball first and then the turf. This drill will improve your contact and thus your control. Lay a piece of string, a small branch, or another object approximately 1 foot long on the ground perpendicular to you. Take your stance so that the string runs directly out from your non-target-side foot. Place a golf ball in the middle of your stance. From this position, execute the pitch shot, concentrating on getting the clubhead past the string before it contacts the ball (figure 4.2). Repeat 10 times.

To Decrease Difficulty

- Use a high-lofted wedge (56 to 60 degrees) and open the clubface.

To Increase Difficulty

- Pitch to targets at 15, 20, and 25 yards (14, 18, and 23 meters).
- Use different wedges (pitching, sand, lob).
- Move the string so that it is only a couple of inches from the ball.

Success Check

- Weight should be on the target-side foot at contact.
- Execute the shot in a relaxed, rhythmic manner.

Score Your Success

Club strikes the ground on the target side of string = 1 point

Club strikes the ball first, then the ground = 2 points

Your score ___

Figure 4.2 String drill.

Pitch Shot Drill 2. *See the Spot*

This drill is designed to help you contact the ball before the ground. Pitch the ball to the practice green (no specific target is needed). Before looking up to see the ball in flight, locate the spot where the ball was before you struck it. Once you see the spot, look up to see where your shot landed. Repeat 10 times.

To Increase Difficulty

• Pick a landing target before executing the shot. Hit the shot, locate the spot the ball occupied before being struck, and then look up to see how close the ball comes to your target.

Success Check

• Weight should be on the target-side foot at contact.

• Execute the shot in a relaxed, rhythmic manner.

Score Your Success

Locate the spot where ball was before looking up = 1 point each shot

Your score ___

Pitch Shot Drill 3. *Target Towel*

Distance control is vital to a successful pitch. You must be able to land the ball on a specific target on the green so that it can roll to the hole. This drill is designed to help you develop this vital touch. Remember, distance control is achieved by regulating the length of the backswing, not by changing the speed of the swing.

Place golf towels at 20, 40, and 60 yards (18, 37, and 55 meters). From a good lie, pitch 10 balls to each target in turn, beginning with the nearest

target towel (figure 4.3). Try to land the ball on the target. Give yourself 5 points if the ball lands on the target, 3 points if the ball lands within 10 yards of the target, and 1 point if the ball comes to rest on or within 10 yards of the target. Hit 10 pitch shots to each target for a total of 30 pitch shots.

To Decrease Difficulty

• Place one golf towel at 25 yards. When you are able to consistently land 5 balls out of 10 within 10 yards of this target, return to the original drill.

• Put the ball on a tee before hitting the pitch shot.

To Increase Difficulty

• Pitch the balls from slight or moderate rough. Pitch shots are often hit from these conditions.

• Pitch the balls with your eyes closed.

Success Check

• Play the ball from the middle of your stance.

• Regulate distance by changing the length of the backswing, not by changing the speed of the swing.

Figure 4.3 Target towel drill.

Score Your Success

25 points or fewer = 5 points

26 to 50 points = 10 points

51 to 75 points = 15 points

76 to 100 points = 20 points

101 to 125 points = 25 points

126 to 150 points = 30 points

Your score ___

Pitch Shot Drill 4. *Pitch and Putt Practice*

Place a golf ball approximately 15 yards (14 meters) from the edge of a practice green and 30 yards (27 meters) from the hole on the practice green. Pitch the ball to the green and then putt the ball into the hole. The goal is to take the fewest number of strokes to hole the ball. Give yourself 20 points if you hole the pitch shot, 10 points if you use a pitch shot and a putt, 5 points if you use a pitch shot and two putts, and 1 point if you use a pitch shot and three putts. Repeat five times.

To Decrease Difficulty

• Place the ball 5 yards (4.5 meters) from the green in a good lie.

• Instead of a hole, pitch and putt to a club or umbrella placed on the green.

To Increase Difficulty

• For each pitch and putt, select a new hole and distance.

• Repeat the drill using a lob wedge, sand wedge, and pitching wedge.

Success Check

• Maintain the spine angle throughout the swing.

• At the finish, weight should be on the target side of the body and the elbows should be high.

Score Your Success

25 points or fewer = 5 points

26 to 50 points = 10 points

51 to 75 points = 15 points

76 to 100 points = 20 points

Your score ___

Pitch Shot Drill 5. *Pitch and Putt Stroke Play*

Select nine holes on a practice green. Place a golf ball approximately 10 yards from the edge of the practice green but in line with the target hole; no other holes should be between your ball and the target hole. Pitch the ball to the green and then putt the ball into the hole. Repeat until you have played all nine holes, taking each hole in turn.

Success Check

• Maintain the spine angle throughout the swing.

• At the finish, weight should be on the target side of the body and the elbows should be high.

Score Your Success

Complete all nine holes in 36 strokes or more = 5 points

Complete all nine holes in 31 to 35 strokes = 10 points

Complete all nine holes in 26 to 30 strokes = 15 points

Complete all nine holes in 25 strokes or fewer = 20 points

Your score ___

Pitch Shot Drill 6. *Pitch and Putt Match Play*

Once you've completed pitch and putt stroke play, get a partner and play a match of nine holes. Begin 10 to 15 yards away from the practice green and select a golf hole on the practice green. Both of you should pitch your ball to the hole and then putt out. The golfer who has the fewest strokes to the hole wins the hole. If you both take the same number of strokes, the hole is halved. Repeat until you have completed all nine holes.

Success Check

- Maintain the spine angle throughout the swing.
- At the finish, weight should be on the target side of the body and the elbows should be high.

Score Your Success

Give yourself 2 points for every hole you win, 1 point for each hole that is halved.

Your score ___

Pitch Shot Drill 7. *Hazard Drill*

A pitch shot is often used to stroke the ball high over a hazard—water, tall rough, a small tree, or a bunker—and make the ball land softly on the green. Golfers often find a pitch shot over a large hazard quite challenging, so the hazard drill allows you to practice your technique under conditions similar to those on a course.

Find a practice green that has a hazard, preferably a sand bunker, nearby (figure 4.4). You should be at least 25 yards from the green. Place 10 golf

Figure 4.4 Hazard drill.

balls a few feet from the hazard. Pitch the balls to the middle of the green.

Once you are comfortable with the pitch shot, try pitching 10 balls over a green-side hazard to a golf hole or target.

To Decrease Difficulty

- Replace the hazard with your golf bag. Place the bag upright between you and the practice green and pitch 10 balls over the bag and onto the green.

To Increase Difficulty

- Pitch the balls to specific target holes.
- Place the golf balls 50 yards (46 meters) from the green-side hazard.
- Hit each of the 10 pitch shots from a different distance.
- Use a different wedge for each shot.

Success Check

- Build shot speed slowly so that the club accelerates through the ball.
- The club should follow the ball toward the target.
- At the finish, weight should be on the target-side foot and the elbows should be high.

Score Your Success

Ball lands and remains on green = 2 points each shot

Your score ___

PITCHING STRATEGY

The first key to pitching strategy is knowing when to hit the pitch shot. The second key is deciding where to land the ball. The pitch shot requires accuracy, so choosing a clear, precise target for the ball is an important strategic decision.

Because a chip permits greater accuracy and control, it is preferred over a pitch. There are, however, occasions when it may be wiser to pitch than to chip. Due to the ball flight characteristics of a pitch shot—high trajectory and little roll—a pitch is a good choice when the hole is close to the edge of the green. A pitch may also be the shot of choice if significantly more carry than roll is desired. For example, if a golfer has 40 yards of fairway and 10 yards of green to get the ball to the hole, a pitch shot is probably the way to go. Finally, when an obstacle, such as a bunker, deep rough, or water, lies between the ball and the green, you should use a pitch shot because it will carry the ball over the obstacle and stop it near the hole. Keep in mind that it takes a great deal of practice to develop the distance control necessary for an effective pitch shot.

In short, consider a chip shot when you have a poor lie or a downhill lie, the green is hard, there is a lot of wind, or you are under stress. Consider a pitch shot when you have a good lie or an uphill lie, the green is soft, or an obstacle is in the way.

The second strategic decision is where to land the ball before it rolls to the hole. If the pitch shot is played to clear an obstacle, then the target should be sufficiently far from the obstacle to ensure that the ball does not land in the trouble area. The purpose of the shot is to simply get the ball on the green. In some cases, this may mean selecting a landing target that is at or even past the hole. The player must ensure that the next shot after a pitch is no worse than a putt. Too often players get greedy when attempting to clear an obstacle and choose a landing target that just clears the hazard, and with a slight mishit they find their ball in the hazard they were attempting to clear. It is wiser to choose a landing target that takes the ball comfortably clear of the trouble.

If you choose the pitch because the ball has to carry more of the fairway or rough but doesn't have to roll so much on the green, a good target is the hole itself. In other words, try to land the ball directly in the hole. Due to slight mishits, most golfers tend to land shots shorter than they intended, and few amateur players hit the ball past the hole even when they try. Choosing the hole as the target ensures that even though the ball may land a little short or a little long, it is still somewhere near the hole; a properly struck pitch shot does not produce much ball roll once it hits the green. However, do not use the hole as the target if it is too close to a hazard or a danger spot. A successful golfer avoids trouble on the golf course.

Pitching Strategy Drill 1. *Chip or Pitch?*

Place 10 balls approximately 5 yards from the edge of a practice green. Pick out one hole and chip five balls. Now pitch five balls to the hole. Which stroke consistently gets the ball closer?

Place 10 balls 5 yards apart in a line moving away from the practice green. The first ball should be 5 yards from the green and the last ball should be 50 yards from the green. Select a hole near the middle of the practice green. Decide if the shot calls for a pitch or chip, select the appropriate club, and pitch or chip the 10 balls to this hole.

To Increase Difficulty

- Pitch and chip from 20 yards away from the green.
- Pitch and chip from 20 yards away with a hazard between you and the green.

Success Check

- Consider the lie and landing area before each shot.

Score Your Success

For the second part of the drill, give yourself 3 points for every shot within 5 yards of the target hole.

Your score ___

Pitching Strategy Drill 2. *Mission Impossible*

This drill is one of the most popular drills with the players on the Swedish national team. With a partner or opponent, select a spot within 50 yards of a practice green that offers a challenging (impossible) shot to the green. Both of you should play a ball from this spot into the hole. The player to hole the ball in the fewest strokes wins the hole. If you both take the same number of strokes for a hole, the hole is halved. Play six holes.

To Decrease Difficulty

- Place the balls within 25 yards of the practice green.

Success Check

- Assess the lie, hazards, wind, and other pertinent factors before each shot.

Score Your Success

Halve the hole = 3 points

Win the hole = 5 points

Your score ___

PITCHING SUCCESS SUMMARY

If you learn to pitch the ball successfully, you will lower your scores. Pitching is fun. To throw the ball high into the air and have it land softly on the green gives a feeling of success and provides excellent practice for the full swing. However, the pitch is not an easy shot. It requires sound mechanics and dedicated practice to develop the necessary touch to execute it properly. Fortunately it is an easy shot to practice because it doesn't require much room or even a regular practice area; a backyard or local park will do.

Review the fundamentals in this chapter, practice the drills, and you will soon notice a difference in the rest of your golf shots. You will also see smaller numbers on your scorecard.

Record your point totals from each of the drills in this step and add them together. If you scored at least 120 out of 218 points, you're ready for the next step. If you scored fewer than 120 points, review the drills that gave you the most trouble before you move on to the next step.

Pitch Shot Drills

1. String Drill		___ out of 20
2. See the Spot		___ out of 10
3. Target Towel		___ out of 30
4. Pitch and Putt Practice		___ out of 20
5. Pitch and Putt Stroke Play		___ out of 20
6. Pitch and Putt Match Play		___ out of 18
7. Hazard Drill		___ out of 40

Pitching Strategy Drills

1. Chip or Pitch?		___ out of 30
2. Mission Impossible		___ out of 30
Total		___ **out of 218**

Almost 75 percent of all shots in a round of golf are fewer than 100 yards from the hole, so the success of your short game largely determines your success overall. With the completion of this step, you have learned the skills and strategies of the short game: putting, chipping, and pitching. When you find yourself within 100 yards of a golf hole, you now know what to do and how to do it. The next logical step is to get from the tee to the green. To successfully launch the ball off the tee or to hit an approach to the green from the fairway requires a single skill, the full golf swing.

Taking a Full Swing

For a proficient golfer, the full swing includes a wide variety of swings. For example, a golfer might execute a full swing with a driver or another wood to play the ball as far as possible. In another situation, the golfer might take a full swing with a sand iron or lob wedge to play the ball high in the air and stop it quickly on the green. A golfer must be able to adapt to the situation at hand and determine what club and shot to hit (see step 9 for tips on choosing the right club).

During a round of golf, the ball is bound to end up in a number of different lies. Playing the game effectively means developing ways to deal with each and every one of those lies. Research shows that experts have more ways to execute a shot from a given lie than players who are less skilled. A good start is to develop a basic full swing that you can manipulate when needed.

On many of the oldest courses in England and Scotland, there are no driving ranges. Golf was and is a game played on a course; with no driving ranges, players have to spend all their time playing and practicing on the course. This means they learn golf skills in gamelike conditions. Since driving ranges are the place most players go to learn golf, there is a huge risk that the skills will not transfer to the course. Practicing only at the driving range, a player simply will not learn how to master all the different situations that occur when playing a course. If you practice only from a good lie on flat ground using a full swing, you will improve only under those conditions. In this step, you will not only learn the full swing, you also will learn to practice in gamelike conditions that will help you become a better overall player.

EXECUTING THE FULL SWING

Preparation for the full swing includes many of the details mentioned in step 2. The grip should allow you to freely swing the club with your hands, arms, and body. You must hold the club with your fingers, not in the palm of your hand.

Choose from an overlap grip, interlocking grip, or baseball grip (figure 5.1). In an overlap grip, the little finger of the right hand overlaps between the index and middle finger of the left hand. The overlap grip is also called the Vardon grip after its inventor, Harry Vardon. In an interlocking grip, the little finger of the right hand interlocks with the index finger of the left hand. In a baseball grip, the hands are separated a bit but close to each other. Experiment with all three to discover which grip works best for you.

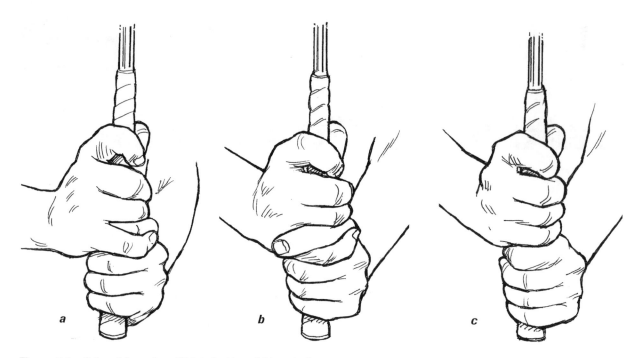

Figure 5.1   Grips: *(a)* overlap; *(b)* interlocking; *(c)* baseball.

The overlap grip is the most common grip. The baseball grip can be a good choice for juniors or players with small hands since having all 10 fingers on the grip may increase the feeling of strength. Small hands may be a disadvantage with the interlocking grip. The hands need to be able to come up on top of the grip (note the two knuckles as described in step 2 on page 20).

The stance or address for a successful full swing contains a few vital elements (figure 5.2). The ball is typically in the middle of the stance;

a general rule is that when you are playing a 6-iron or higher, the ball should be in the middle of the stance. When playing a wedge, the ball can be even farther back if you feel this will give you cleaner contact with the ball. The ball may be forward in the stance toward the target-side foot if you are using a longer club such as a low iron or wood. With a 5-iron, you can move the ball slightly forward of center, and for each club lower, move the ball a bit more forward. However, the ball should never be ahead of

Figure 5.2   Correct address position.

the inside heel of the forward foot. Feet should be shoulder-width apart and weight should be equally distributed between the right and left foot and between the toe and heel of each foot. The feet, hips, and shoulders are parallel with the target line. The knees are slightly bent, with the hips slightly flexed and the arms hanging freely in front of the body. The hands grip the club in a relaxed way.

Once you have achieved the proper address, the next step is the actual swing. Think of the swing in three phases:

1. Backswing, including the takeaway
2. Downswing, including contact with the ball
3. Follow-through

Some players start the backswing with a forward press (figure 5.3a). In a forward press, the hands, arms, and right knee act as a trigger to start the takeaway. For the most part, using a forward press is individual preference. Say you are supposed to jump up from a position with your knees slightly bent. Will you feel more comfortable jumping by merely extending your legs? Or will you feel more comfortable if you quickly flex your legs before extending them? Most people find the latter option more comfortable since it uses the stretch-shortening effect. They feel stronger when they flex slightly before jumping. Some players feel the same way about the golf swing and the forward press.

Another reason to try the forward press is that some players aren't certain when and how

to start the backswing. With a forward press, the start of the backswing becomes more of a reaction to the forward movement caused by the forward press. However, some players feel more at ease starting the backswing by moving away from the ball. Try both options and stick to what feels best for you.

The backswing (figure 5.3b) begins as the triangle of hands and shoulders move with the left hip and knee to bring the clubhead straight back. Weight shifts to the heel of the inside foot (right foot for a right-handed hitter). The right knee stays bent. The shoulders turn about 90 degrees until the left shoulder comes under the chin, allowing the club shaft to move into a position parallel with the ground. The left arm stays reasonably straight.

The start of the downswing (figure 5.3c) is a crucial part of the full swing. The start of the downswing determines both the path the club will take and the position of the clubface through impact with the ball. The downswing is a movement that points downward and forward. As the club moves down toward the ball, the body weight moves forward toward the front foot (left foot for a right-handed golfer). This is called the magic move. If you are swinging with an iron, the club should hit the ball and then the ground, leaving a divot after the ball. Think about starting the downswing by letting the weight shift to the front foot and bringing the heel to the ground while at the same time bringing the right elbow back down toward the body.

Misstep

During the takeaway, you lift the club off the ball using your hands and arms.

Correction

Make sure your hands and shoulders work together during the takeaway. Try the belly-button backswing drill (page 58).

Misstep

At the top of the backswing, body weight is on the left foot, making the body look like a backward C.

Correction

This error occurs when you do not shift your weight to the right foot or straighten the right knee. Body weight should be on the inside right heel and the right knee should still be bent at the top of the backswing. Try the back-tapping drill (page 59).

Figure 5.3 | Executing the Full Swing

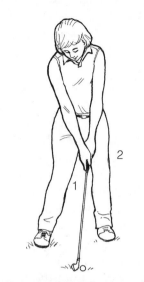

a

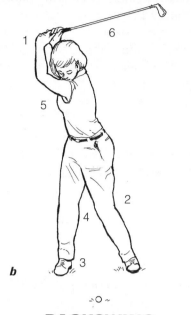

b

FORWARD PRESS

1. Use as a trigger to the takeaway
2. Press with the hands, arms, and right knee (right-handed golfer)

BACKSWING

1. Beginning with the triangle of hands and shoulders, take the clubhead away from the ball
2. The left knee and hip should follow as the clubhead moves straight back the first few inches
3. Shift your weight to the inside right heel
4. Bend the right knee
5. Turn the shoulders about 90 degrees until the left shoulder is under the chin
6. Move the shaft so that it is parallel with ground as the left arm is straight

If the backswing and downswing work the way they should, the follow-through (figure 5.3d) is easy. If you have a good follow-through, chances are your backswing and downswing are good because the follow-through is a result of what has gone before. Body weight should now be on a flat left foot with the body in an erect position and the club resting on the left shoulder. The follow-through position should be comfortable to hold. The body should feel balanced and you shouldn't feel like you are about to fall over.

Misstep

You find it difficult to stay in the follow-through position.

Correction

You may be distributing your weight incorrectly at address or starting the backswing too quickly. Try the finish drill (page 61), focusing on finding a comfortable follow-through.

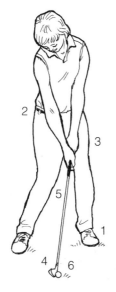

c

d

DOWNSWING

1. Shift your weight to the left foot while the right elbow comes back down to the body
2. Use a smooth downswing to increase speed
3. Release the clubhead
4. At impact, the clubhead should be square to the target
5. Turn the back of the left hand to the target
6. The clubhead should hit ball and then cut a divot in the ground

FOLLOW-THROUGH

1. Your weight should be on the flat left foot
2. Keep the body erect, not bent
3. Rest the club on the left shoulder and behind the back
4. The final position should be comfortable to hold

Misstep

You hit on top of the ball, resulting in no ball flight.

Correction

This error can be the result of a number of faults: ending up on the wrong foot at impact, not shifting weight at the start of the downswing, or the misconception that the player should lift the ball up in the air (ball flight should instead be created by the loft of the club). Use full swing drills 4, 5, and 6 (pages 60-62) to reinforce the weight shift and attack on the ball.

Full Swing Drill 1. *Forward Press*

Set up to a ball as if you are about to play a shot. Try a forward press, using the hands, arms, or right knee (right-handed golfer). Immediately start the backswing after the forward press. Try to start the backswing without a forward press on every second swing, and note which style feels most comfortable. Complete each start by swinging the club all the way back to the top of the backswing. Take a total of 20 swings, 10 with a forward press and 10 without, trying to complete the backswing with your weight shifting to your rear foot. Give yourself 1 point for each completed backswing with or without the forward press. Give yourself 2 points if you complete the backswing with your weight mostly on the rear foot.

To Decrease Difficulty

- Swing the club only halfway through the backswing, focusing solely on the start of the swing.
- Stand in front of a mirror and watch yourself as you perform the backswing.

To Increase Difficulty

- Slowly continue the swing, bringing the club down to the point at which the club would hit the ball. Stop and notice your position.
- Continue the swing through the downswing and try to hit the ground with the clubhead.
- Complete the swing to the finish position.

Success Check

- Complete the forward press with the hands, arms, or right knee.
- Shift your weight to the rear foot during the backswing.

Score Your Success

0 to 6 points = 0 points

7 to 12 points = 1 point

13 to 19 points = 2 points

20 to 26 points = 3 points

27 to 33 points = 4 points

34 to 40 points = 5 points

Your score ___

Full Swing Drill 2. *Belly-Button Backswing*

Grip down the shaft of the club and take a normal stance. Touch your belly button with the butt of the grip. Feel the one-piece takeaway as you start the backswing with the triangle of hands and shoulders. Let your body rotate and allow the weight to shift to your rear foot. Start the swing and go halfway back on the shoulder turn. Take 10 swings, scoring yourself based on the following criteria:

- Butt of grip loses contact with your belly button at the start of the backswing = 0 points
- Butt of grip loses contact with your belly button shortly after the start of the swing = 1 point

- Club stays in contact with your belly button as the shoulders turn halfway = 2 points
- Shoulders turn halfway, the club stays in contact with your belly button, and weight shifts to the rear foot = 3 points

To Decrease Difficulty

- Focus only on the first few inches of the swing. Try to get a feel for how the backswing starts with the arms, hands, and shoulders moving together.

58

To Increase Difficulty

- Grip farther up the shaft and do not let the butt of the grip contact your belly button, but keep the grip pointing at your belly button as you start the swing.
- Grip the club as you normally would, take a normal stance, and try to execute the same kind of one-piece takeaway.

Success Check

- Slowly execute the takeaway with the arms, shoulders, and hands working as a triangle.
- Move your weight to the inside right heel.

Score Your Success

0 to 5 points = 0 points

6 to 10 points = 1 point

11 to 15 points = 2 points

16 to 20 points = 3 points

21 to 25 points = 4 points

26 to 30 points = 5 points

Your score ___

Full Swing Drill 3. *Back-Tapping*

Take a normal address position, execute a backswing (with or without a forward press, whatever feels right for you), and stop at the top of the backswing. With your eyes still focused on the ball, gently let go of the club and notice where it falls. The shaft of the club should hit your shoulder or right biceps (right-handed golfer). Take a total of 10 swings and give yourself points based on the following criteria:

- Club doesn't come to the top of the backswing = 0 points
- Club comes to the top of the backswing, eyes lose focus on the ball = 1 point
- Club comes to the top of the backswing, eyes stay focused on ball, club falls behind the body = 2 points
- Club comes to the top of the backswing, eyes stay focused on ball, club hits the shoulder or right biceps = 3 points
- Club comes to the top of the backswing, eyes stay focused on the ball, club hits the shoulder or right biceps, weight is on the rear foot = 4 points

To Decrease Difficulty

- Let your eyes follow the club back and adjust your position at the top of the backswing so that the club falls on your shoulder or right biceps.

- Stand in front of a mirror and adjust to the image you see.

To Increase Difficulty

- Have a friend check your backswing position. Complete the full swing instead of stopping at the top of the backswing.
- Hit balls as a friend watches the top of your backswing position.

Success Check

- Set up in a normal stance that feels comfortable and grip the club.
- Swing the club back and at the same time let your weight shift to the inside heel of the rear foot.
- Keep your focus on the ball.

Score Your Success

0 to 6 points = 0 points

7 to 13 points = 1 point

14 to 20 points = 2 points

21 to 27 points = 3 points

28 to 34 points = 4 points

35 to 40 points = 5 points

Your score ___

Full Swing Drill 4. *The Magic Move*

Take a normal address position, but instead of using a ball put a tee in the ground where the ball would go. Swing the club back and start the downswing by shifting your weight to the left foot as you bring the right elbow back down to your body (the magic move). Focus on the left foot and make sure you rest your heel firmly on the ground (right-handed golfer).

As you continue the downswing, keep in mind what the finish position feels and looks like and try to reach that position instead of thinking about swinging the club down to the ball. Focus on clipping the tee at impact. If you run into problems with your downswing, try to watch a good player at the club or on TV. Pay attention to what the player does. Note especially how the club attacks the ball in a downward motion as the body weight shifts to the target-side foot.

The goal is to clip the tee at impact. Start with a lot of tee above the ground and as you progress, press the tee deeper into the ground. Be sure to clip the tee before you hit the ground. Take a total of 10 swings and give yourself points based on the following criteria:

- Swing back, start the downswing, but do not shift weight to the forward foot = 0 points
- Swing back, start the downswing with the magic move and right elbow = 1 point
- Swing with the magic move to the finish position but miss the tee = 2 points
- Swing correctly using the magic move and clip the tee = 3 points
- Swing correctly using the magic move, clip the tee, and hit the ground = 4 points

To Decrease Difficulty

- Use a tall tee and focus only on clipping the tee.
- Use a long club or a wood at first to make it easier to reach the tee.

To Increase Difficulty

- Press the tee deeper into the ground. Be sure to clip the tee and then hit the ground.
- Take away the tee and use a ball instead. Hit the ball and then the ground (make a divot).

Success Check

- Set up comfortably to the tee in a relaxed position.
- Swing back and shift your weight to the rear foot.
- Start the downswing with the magic move and complete the swing to the finish position.

Score Your Success

0 to 6 points = 0 points

7 to 13 points =1 point

14 to 20 points =2 points

21 to 27 points = 3 points

28 to 34 points = 4 points

35 to 40 points = 5 points

Your score ____

Full Swing Drill 5. *Right Foot, Left Foot*

Set up in a normal address position. Without using a ball, swing back and at the same time lift the forward foot (left foot for a right-handed golfer) off the ground. Swing down and through as you bring the forward foot back to the ground and lift the rear foot off the ground. Place a ball in front of you and hit it to a target using the same technique. Hit a total of 10 balls and give yourself points based on the following criteria:

- Swing back, lift the forward foot off the ground but lose balance = 0 points
- Swing back, lift the forward foot, swing through, lift the rear foot but lose balance = 1 point
- Swing back and forward, lift both feet, miss the ball = 2 points
- Swing back and forward in good balance and hit the ball = 3 points
- Swing back and forward in good balance and hit the ball to the target = 4 points

To Decrease Difficulty

- Put the ball on a tee and use a long club.
- Put the ball on a tee and use a short club.

To Increase Difficulty

- Put two or more balls in a row and hit them one after another. Take a short break between the two balls.
- Put up to five balls in a row and hit them one after another without stopping between shots. Slowly move forward to hit the next ball in line.

Success Check

- Get a nice rhythm going by taking a few practice swings. Move the rear foot and then the forward foot.
- Focus on your balance and do not swing too hard.

Score Your Success

0 to 6 points = 0 points

7 to 13 points = 1 point

14 to 20 points = 2 points

21 to 27 points = 3 points

28 to 34 points = 4 points

35 to 40 points = 5 points

Your score ___

Full Swing Drill 6. *The Finish*

Set up to play a shot but don't use a ball. Instead of swinging the club back, swing it forward to your intended finish position. Be sure the club is in a position that feels comfortable. Your weight is on the left foot and your body is erect. Check your balance and allow your body to feel the position.

Take a swing and try to finish in the position you just practiced. Compare the positions, adjust, and try again. When you feel you can get to the comfortable position without a ball, try the same thing with a ball. Hit a total of 10 shots and give yourself points based on the following criteria:

- Difficult to find a balanced finish position = 0 points

- Balance comfortably in the finish position = 1 point
- Swing back, forward, and finish in balance = 2 points
- Swing back, hit the ball, and finish in balance = 3 points
- Swing back, hit the ball, and find the perfect finish = 4 points

To Decrease Difficulty

- Take a practice swing or find the finish position without the ball between each shot.
- Take away the ball and focus only on the swing. Try to hit the ground when swinging.

61

To Increase Difficulty

- Change clubs after each shot.
- Change clubs and lies, trying the drill from uphill, downhill, and sidehill lies.

Success Check

- Draw a clear blueprint in your mind of the perfect finish position and work on developing muscle memory.
- Focus on reaching the balanced finish position during every shot. When you do, the rest will take care of itself.

FULL SWING STRATEGY

Hitting shots with a full swing involves strategic thinking. First, ask yourself what you want to do with the shot. As you develop skill, strategic concerns such as ball flight, right or left turn, and high or low trajectory become more and more important.

New golfers spend most of their strategy time finding a target and picking a club simply because the number of ways they can hit a shot is limited. Professional players, on the other hand, take all aspects of the shot into account. Wind, lie, slopes, hazards, pin position, green firmness, individual preferences, and other factors all help the professional player decide on ball flight.

For example, PGA-tour player Jesper Parnevik was once faced with an interesting strategic decision while on his way to winning the Byron Nelson Golf Classic in Dallas. Jesper was standing on the 17th tee, a par-3 hole with the pin far back on the right-hand side of the green. To the right of the green was a water hazard, but to the left of the pin the green was wide open. All the external clues pointed to the conclusion that the best shot would move from left to right, stopping the ball left of the pin and completely avoiding the water. However, Jesper felt more comfortable hitting a shot that moved from right to left, a much more difficult shot under the circumstances. Even so, he hit the shot, put

the ball on the green, and walked away with the tournament win.

As you develop as a player, the answer to the question of what to do with the ball will become a matter of adjusting to the conditions set by the golf course and by yourself. The better player you are, the more answers you will find and the more variety your shots will have.

Once you've decided what you want to do, consider how you will get it done, investigating your ability to perform the necessary shot. A good player is able to create the best shot for any given situation. Consider again the example of Jesper Parnevik. He probably knew that the best shot was not a high draw (moving right to left), but his confidence in hitting such a shot was so much greater, he decided to hit it anyway. Hitting a fade that moved left to right might have ended up in water and led to a disastrous finish. On the other hand, if Jesper wanted to become an even better player, he would learn to hit a fade shot even in pressure situations. There may come a time when that is the only shot to play.

Before you can reach Jesper Parnevik's level, the most important answer to the question "How?" is simply the technique you need to produce the shot. A straight forward shot may require your regular full swing. For softer ball flight, perhaps a smoother swing with a longer club could do the trick.

It isn't easy to practice strategic thinking for a full swing without playing on a golf course. A driving range or practice area usually looks different from the course. Practicing under game-like conditions will help you transfer what you learn in practice to the golf course.

Full Swing Strategy Drill 1. *Hit the Target*

On the driving range, pick a target for your shot, such as a sign, a different colored spot on the ground, or a group of balls lying on the fairway. Your goal is to hit the target, but on every shot decide on an area around the target about the size of a green. Play at least 20 shots with different clubs and give yourself 1 point every time you hit the green area.

To Decrease Difficulty

- Make your visualized area of the green bigger.
- Use all clubs in the bag all the way up to the driver.

To Increase Difficulty

- Make your visualized area of the green smaller.

- Use only the 8-iron up to the wedge.

Success Check

- Focus on the target and let your swing take care of itself.

Score Your Success

0 to 2 greens hit = 0 points

3 to 5 greens hit = 1 point

6 to 8 greens hit = 2 points

9 to 11 greens hit = 3 points

12 to 14 greens hit = 4 points

15 to 20 greens hit = 5 points

Your score ___

Full Swing Strategy Drill 2. *Parnevik Drill*

Jesper likes to curve his shots. Fade, draw, high, and low are types of trajectories he uses all the time. Take 10 balls, and before each shot, decide on a target and the type of shot you want to hit. For example, try to hit the 100-yard (91-meter) marker with a fade shot. What club will do the job? How will you swing? Give yourself 1 point every time you hit the target (within what you think is an acceptable distance) and 2 points every time you get the ball flight and trajectory right and hit the target.

To Decrease Difficulty

- Use the same club for all 10 shots and vary only the trajectory.
- Hit three draws in a row, then three fades, three high, and so on.

To Increase Difficulty

- Change clubs and targets for every shot.
- Vary the distances using long clubs to short clubs.

Success Check

- Make sure you have a clear idea of what to do and how to do it.

Score Your Success

0 to 2 points = 0 points

3 to 5 points = 1 point

6 to 8 points = 2 points

9 to 11 points = 3 points

12 to 14 points = 4 points

15 to 20 points = 5 points

Your score ___

FULL SWING SUCCESS SUMMARY

Developing a sound full swing is fundamental to playing successful golf. A good player does not necessary use the full swing as a straightforward shot during tournament play, but every swing is some sort of manipulation of the basic swing based on the conditions at hand.

The full swing has three phases: backswing, downswing, and follow-through. You can execute a full swing with nearly any club in the bag. Strategic thinking for the full swing involves understanding club selection, knowing how to hit different types of shots, and adjusting to the ever-changing conditions on a golf course.

Record your point totals from each of the drills in this step and add them together. A score of 30 points or more indicates you have mastered this step and are ready to move on to the next. A score of 18 to 25 points is adequate, and you should be able to move to the next step after reviewing and practicing the drills in which you scored low. If you scored fewer than 18 points, review and practice the drills a few more times before you move on to the next step.

Full Swing Drills

1. Forward Press	___ out of 5
2. Belly-Button Backswing	___ out of 5
3. Back-Tapping	___ out of 5
4. The Magic Move	___ out of 5
5. Right Foot, Left Foot	___ out of 5
6. The Finish	___ out of 5

Full Swing Strategy Drills

1. Hit the Target	___ out of 5
2. Parnevik Drill	___ out of 5
Total	___ *out of 40*

A golf course is ever changing with varying slopes, different lengths of grass, hazards, and trees to make the round more interesting and challenging. Now that you have mastered the full swing and have a basic understanding of how to strategically adjust to different conditions, you are ready to take your swing to the course, which will test your ability with a number of lies. Sidehill lies, uphill lies, downhill lies, and other types of bad lies are waiting for you in the next step, so move ahead to learn how to master those shots.

Overcoming a Difficult Lie

Someone once said that playing golf on a golf course is like being an artist who has to come up with a new idea for every painting. In a round of golf, you'll probably never have two lies that are the same, except perhaps when playing from the tee box. A golf course has slopes that result in uneven lies—uphill, downhill, and sidehill—and obstructions such as trees, grass of different lengths, and hazards.

To play golf successfully, you must be able to adjust your swing and strategy to these different conditions. Unlike many other sports, golf usually is practiced in a different environment from the one in which it is played. Hitting balls on a driving range usually means standing on a mat or a flat practice fairway, which does not offer a chance to practice the uneven lies you are most likely to come across on the course.

A good lie occurs when the ball comes to rest in a nice, flat, grassy area, much like the driving range. A bad lie is more likely to occur than a good lie and may be the uphill, downhill, or sidehill lie that most players spend their time reacting to on the golf course. A bad lie can also mean finding your ball in an old divot, in thick rough, or behind a tree. Depending on how skilled you are, you will find your share of good and bad lies and the only thing you can do is develop ways to handle the different lies you will face.

One of golf's greatest of all time, Severiano Ballesteros, was famous for the way he treated a bad lie. He was not the greatest driver so he found himself in the woods, in thick grass, or facing other obstructions from time to time. However, like nobody else he could find his way out and very often onto the green and even close to the pin. His victory in the British Open from the parking lot on the last hole is a classic.

The location of the ball relative to your feet when you set up to hit the ball defines the type of lie. In a sidehill lie, the ball is either above or below your feet (figure 6.1). In an uphill or downhill lie, the ball is even with your feet but the slope it is resting on puts your feet at different levels (figure 6.2). The target-side foot is either higher (uphill) or lower (downhill) than the rear foot.

Figure 6.1 Sidehill lies: *(a)* ball above feet; *(b)* ball below feet.

Figure 6.2 *(a)* Uphill and *(b)* downhill lies.

UNEVEN-LIE ADJUSTMENTS

There are many ways to adjust to an uneven lie. Ball position, weight distribution, grip, alignment, swing length, and club selection are important factors to consider when adjusting to the terrain. Hitting a 5-iron from a downhill, uphill, or sidehill lie is different than hitting it from a flat fairway. A good player automatically calculates risk and reward when faced with such a lie. Is it better to select a higher-numbered club to make a clean connection with the ball?

Can you swing with full speed and still keep your balance and proper ball flight? Will the ball curve in any direction because of the slope? The best way to discover what works best for you is to try different lies and observe what the ball does. However, a few guidelines can help. For an uneven lie, the preparation needs to allow for a free swing. With practice you will learn what slope does to the ball, but the suggestions here will help you manage uneven lies.

Uphill and Downhill Lies

When the ball is even with your feet but your feet are on different levels, the club has to have a chance to come down to the ball on the same path as in a shot from flat ground. This means your shoulders must follow, or be parallel with, the level of the ground when you set up to the shot.

When playing from an uphill lie (figure 6.3), the target-side foot is higher than the rear foot, so the first thing to do is to get the shoulders parallel to the ground at setup. This stops the club from coming into the ball at too steep of an angle and still allows for clean contact between the club and the ball. The grip is the same as in a normal shot, although it may help to choke down on the grip a little to get your hands closer to the ball.

The ball can be a bit forward in the stance to make the club's angle of attack slightly shallower.

It is a good idea to step away from the ball, take a couple of practice swings, and note where the club hits the ground relative to your feet; that is where the ball position should be. Since the ball will tend to draw from an uphill lie, modify your alignment so that you aim to the right.

The swing should be no different than a normal swing. Take the club back and let your weight shift to the rear side. You may want to shorten the backswing a fraction to maintain your balance. Because of the slope it will be much easier to shift weight in the backswing, but it will also be more difficult to shift weight to the target side in the downswing and follow-through. At the finish of the swing moving all your weight to the forward foot is going to be more or less impossible, but you should be able to find a position in which you can maintain your balance.

Figure 6.3   Hitting an Uphill Lie

PREPARATION

1. Use the same grip as when hitting a normal full swing

2. Choke up on the grip a little (hands closer to the ball)

3. Use a normal stance with the alignment slightly right of the target

4. Make sure your shoulders are parallel with the slope

5. Evenly distribute your weight on both feet or slightly more on the lower foot

6. Lean into the hill

7. Position the ball slightly toward the target foot

a

(continued)

Figure 6.3 *(continued)*

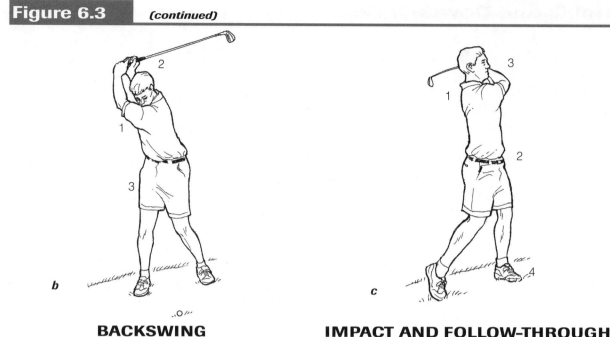

b

c

BACKSWING

1. Start the swing and backswing as in a normal full swing

2. Shorten the backswing a little to maintain balance

3. Shift your weight to the rear side during the backswing

IMPACT AND FOLLOW-THROUGH

1. Start the downswing as in a normal swing

2. Shift your weight to the target side

3. Swing through as in a normal swing

4. Balance at the end with your weight on the target foot

Misstep

When you hit from an uphill or downhill lie, the ball ends up either right or left of the target.

Correction

You are probably aiming at the target, but since the slope causes the ball to curve, you need to adjust your aim. Aim to the right on uphill shots and to the left on downhill shots.

When playing from a downhill lie (figure 6.4), the rear foot is higher than the target foot. Making the shoulders parallel to the ground at setup requires the opposite adjustment of that for an uphill lie. You may feel the weight leans a bit more to the target-side foot, which will help the club achieve a steeper angle of attack. The grip is the same as in a normal shot, except instead of choking down it may be a good idea to leave a bit more grip between the hands and the clubhead.

The ball can be a bit farther back in the stance, again to achieve a steeper angle of attack. Step away from the ball, take a couple of practice swings, and note where the club hits the ground relative to your feet. Use that mark for your ball position. Your alignment should be slightly left of the target since the ball tends to fade.

The swing should be no different than a normal swing. Take the club back and let your weight shift to the rear side, which will be more difficult than in a normal shot. Similar to the uphill lie, you may want to shorten the backswing a fraction to maintain your balance. As you swing through it will be easy to shift weight to the target-side foot. With the ball a bit back in the stance you should be able to make a clean connection. At the finish of the swing, find a position where you can maintain your balance with weight on the target-side foot.

 **Figure 6.4** **Hitting a Downhill Lie**

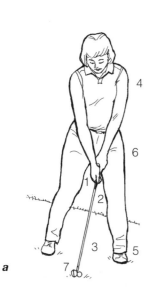

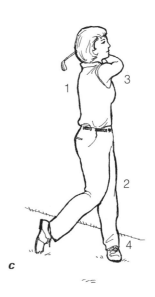

a

b

c

PREPARATION

1. Use the same grip as for a normal full swing

2. Choke up a bit on the grip (hands closer to the ball)

3. Use a normal stance with the alignment slightly left of the target

4. Make sure your shoulders are parallel with the slope

5. Evenly distribute your weight between both feet or place slightly more on the target-side foot

6. Lean into the hill

7. Position the ball slightly toward the high foot

BACKSWING

1. Start the swing and backswing as in a normal full swing

2. Shorten the backswing a little to maintain your balance

3. Shift your weight to the rear side during the backswing

IMPACT AND FOLLOW-THROUGH

1. Start the downswing as in a normal swing

2. Shift your weight to the target side

3. Swing through as in a normal swing

4. Balance at the end with your weight on the target-side foot

Misstep

You hit the top of the ball when hitting from a downhill lie or you hit the ground before you hit the ball (hit the ball fat).

Correction

You probably have too much weight on the high foot or the ball is too close to the low foot. Be sure to finish with your weight on the low foot. Move the ball toward the high foot when you set up.

Sidehill Lies

Like uphill and downhill lies, sidehill lies will also be easier to hit with some slight modifications. In a sidehill lie, the ball is either below or above your feet when you take your stance, which you will need to adjust for when gripping the club and setting up to the ball. When you hit a normal shot from a sidehill lie, the ball is likely to curve in the downward direction of the slope.

When you set up to a sidehill shot where the ball is above your feet (figure 6.5), you may not need to make many changes. Since the ball is above your feet you may want to choke down on the grip a bit so that you don't hit the ground before you hit the ball. Also, the slope may make you put more weight on the heels than in a normal shot. When the ball is above your feet, it will tend to draw or hook as you play the shot. To adjust for that, simply aim to the right. The actual swing is basically a normal swing, though it may be a fraction shorter so that you can maintain balance and you will need to pay attention to the finish of the swing. Balance can be hard to find in a sidehill slope.

Figure 6.5 | Hitting a Sidehill Lie, Ball Above Feet

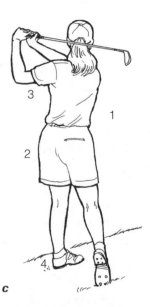

a
b
c

PREPARATION

1. Use the normal grip but choke up a little on the club
2. Use the normal setup but aim slightly right of the target
3. Distribute your weight evenly between both feet or slightly toward the heels
4. Position the ball in the center of the stance or slightly forward, especially when using a longer club

BACKSWING

1. Start the swing and backswing as in a normal full swing
2. Shorten the backswing a little to maintain balance
3. Shift your weight to the rear side during the backswing

IMPACT AND FOLLOW-THROUGH

1. Start the downswing as in a normal swing
2. Shift your weight to the target side
3. Swing through as in a normal swing
4. End in balance with your weight on the target-side foot

Misstep

You hit the ground before you hit the ball (hit the ball fat) when the ball is above your feet.

Correction

You need to make more of an adjustment to the slope. Choke up on the club, shift your weight to your heels, and check the ball position.

Setting up to a sidehill shot where the ball is below your feet (figure 6.6) does not require many changes. Because the ball is below your feet, you may want to use the full length of the grip to prevent you from hitting the ball thin. Putting a bit more weight on the toes will also help you hit the ball accurately. When the ball is below your feet, it will tend to fade or slice as you play the shot, so simply aim to the left. The actual swing is basically a normal swing, except it may be a fraction shorter to help you maintain your balance and you will need to pay attention to the finish of the swing.

Figure 6.6 **Hitting a Sidehill Lie, Ball Below Feet**

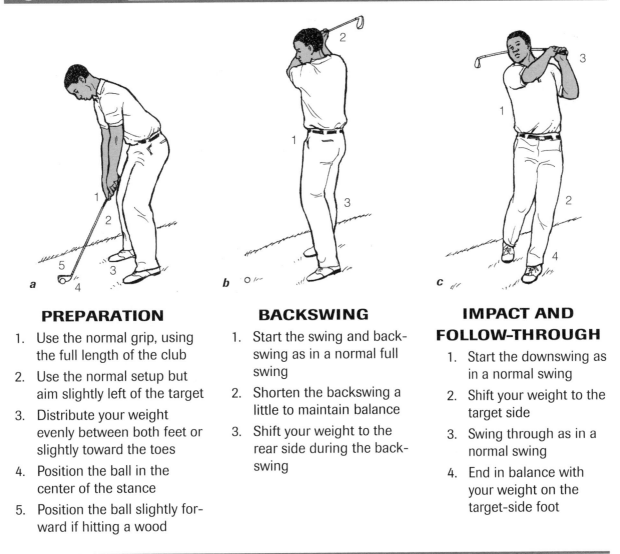

PREPARATION

1. Use the normal grip, using the full length of the club

2. Use the normal setup but aim slightly left of the target

3. Distribute your weight evenly between both feet or slightly toward the toes

4. Position the ball in the center of the stance

5. Position the ball slightly forward if hitting a wood

BACKSWING

1. Start the swing and backswing as in a normal full swing

2. Shorten the backswing a little to maintain balance

3. Shift your weight to the rear side during the backswing

IMPACT AND FOLLOW-THROUGH

1. Start the downswing as in a normal swing

2. Shift your weight to the target side

3. Swing through as in a normal swing

4. End in balance with your weight on the target-side foot

Misstep

With the ball below your feet in a sidehill lie, you hit the top of the ball.

Correction

You need to make more of an adjustment to the slope. Use the full length of the club. Maintain your posture over the ball and make sure you are not sitting back too much on your heels.

Misstep

When you hit a ball from a sidehill lie, the ball ends up right or left of the target.

Correction

You are probably aiming at the target. Since the slope will cause the ball to curve, you need to adjust your aim. Aim left of the target for a sidehill lie with the ball below your feet and aim right of the target for a sidehill lie with the ball above your feet.

Uneven Lie Drill 1. *Find the Ground, Uphill and Downhill Lies*

Find a slope where you can set up to hit uphill and downhill lies. Since you will not hit balls at first, you can use the same slope and face the opposite way without causing danger. Set up to hit a shot, but don't use a ball. Use a 5- or 6-iron. The goal is to hit the ground where the imaginary ball is positioned and to maintain balance throughout the swing. Take 10 swings, 5 uphill and 5 downhill, varying the type of shot as much as you can (uphill lie followed by a downhill lie followed by an uphill lie, for example). Give yourself points for each swing based on the following criteria:

- Lose your balance and miss the ground = 0 points
- Maintain your balance but miss the ground = 1 point
- Hit the ground but lose your balance = 2 points
- Maintain your balance and hit the ground = 3 points

Your goal is to complete 10 swings, 5 uphill and 5 downhill, hitting the ground in the right spot and maintaining balance throughout each swing.

To Decrease Difficulty

- Hit all 5 uphill lies before hitting the 5 downhill lies.
- Use a longer club, such as a 3- or 4-iron, instead of the 5- or 6-iron.

To Increase Difficulty

- Use a shorter club, such as a 9-iron, instead of the 5- or 6-iron.
- Use a different club for each shot.

Success Check

- Adjust your setup and grip to the lie.
- Take a couple of practice swings if you feel uncomfortable. Try to find your balance.

Score Your Success

0 to 4 points = 0 points

5 to 9 points = 1 point

10 to 14 points = 2 points

15 to 19 points = 3 points

20 to 24 points = 4 points

25 points or more = 5 points

Your score ___

Uneven Lie Drill 2. *Clip the Tee, Uphill and Downhill Lies*

This drill is the same as uneven lie drill 1, Find the Ground, but instead of simply using the ground, firmly press a tee into the ground where your imaginary ball is. The goal is to clip the tee and maintain your balance throughout each swing. Take 10 swings, 5 uphill and 5 downhill, varying the type of shot as much as you can (uphill lie followed by a downhill lie followed by an uphill lie, for example). Give yourself points for each swing based on the following criteria:

- Lose your balance and miss the tee = 0 points
- Maintain your balance throughout the swing but miss the tee = 1 point
- Hit the tee but lose your balance = 2 points
- Maintain your balance and hit the tee = 3 points

Your goal is to complete 10 swings, 5 uphill and 5 downhill, clipping the tee and maintaining balance throughout each swing.

To Decrease Difficulty

- Hit all five uphill lies before hitting the five downhill lies.
- Use a longer club, such as a 3- or 4-iron, instead of the 5- or 6-iron.

To Increase Difficulty

- Use a shorter club, such as a 9-iron, instead of the 5- or 6-iron.
- Use a different club for each shot.

Success Check

- Adjust your setup and grip to the lie.
- Take a couple of practice swings if you feel uncomfortable. Try to find your balance.

Score Your Success

0 to 4 points = 0 points

5 to 9 points = 1 point

10 to 14 points = 2 points

15 to 19 points = 3 points

20 to 24 points = 4 points

25 points or more = 5 points

Your score ___

Uneven Lie Drill 3. *Find the Ground, Sidehill Lies*

Find a slope where you can set up for sidehill lies both with the ball below your feet and above your feet. You will not hit balls, so you can use a slope facing the opposite way without causing danger. Set up as if to hit a shot, but without a ball. Use a 5- or 6-iron. The goal is to hit the ground where the imaginary ball is positioned and to maintain your balance throughout the swing. Complete 10 swings, 5 with the imaginary ball above your feet and 5 with it below, varying the type of shot as much as you can (for example, sidehill lie with the ball below the feet followed by a sidehill lie with the ball above the feet). Give yourself points for each swing based on the following criteria:

- Lose your balance and miss the ground = 0 points
- Maintain your balance throughout the swing but miss the ground = 1 point
- Hit the ground but lose your balance = 2 points
- Maintain your balance and hit the ground = 3 points

Your goal is to complete 10 swings, 5 with the imaginary ball above your feet and 5 with it below, hitting the ground in the right spot and maintaining balance throughout each swing.

To Decrease Difficulty

- Hit all 5 sidehill lies with the ball below your feet before you hit the 5 sidehill lies with the ball above your feet.
- Use a longer club, such as a 3- or 4-iron, instead of the 5- or 6-iron.

To Increase Difficulty

- Press a tee into the ground so that only the top shows where the imaginary ball is. Hit the tee when you hit the ground.
- Use a shorter club, such as a 9-iron, instead of the 5- or 6-iron.

Success Check

- Adjust your setup and grip to the lie.
- Take a couple of practice swings if you feel uncomfortable. Try to find your balance.

Score Your Success

0 to 4 points = 0 points

5 to 9 points = 1 point

10 to 14 points = 2 points

15 to 19 points = 3 points

20 to 24 points = 4 points

25 points or more = 5 points

Your score ___

Uneven Lie Drill 4. *Clip the Tee, Sidehill Lies*

This drill is the same as uneven lie drill 3, Find the Ground, but instead of simply trying to find the ground, press a tee firmly into the ground where the imaginary ball is. Try to clip the tee on each shot. Your goal is to hit the tee where the imaginary ball is positioned and to maintain your balance throughout the swing. Complete 10 swings, 5 with the imaginary ball above your feet and 5 with it below, varying the type of shot as much as you can (for example, sidehill lie with the ball below the feet followed by sidehill lie with the ball above the feet). Give yourself points for each swing based on the following criteria:

- Lose your balance and miss the tee = 0 points
- Maintain your balance but miss the tee = 1 point
- Hit the tee but lose your balance = 2 points
- Maintain your balance and hit the tee = 3 points

Your goal is to complete 10 swings, 5 with the imaginary ball above your feet and 5 with it below, hitting the tee in the right spot and maintaining balance throughout each swing.

To Decrease Difficulty

- Hit all 5 sidehill lies with the ball below your feet before you hit the 5 sidehill lies with the ball above your feet.
- Use a longer club, such as a 3- or 4-iron, instead of the 5- or 6-iron.

To Increase Difficulty

- Use a shorter club, such as a 9-iron, instead of the 5- or 6-iron.
- Use a different club on every shot.

Success Check

- Adjust your setup and grip to the lie.
- Take a couple of practice swings if you feel uncomfortable. Try to find your balance.

Score Your Success

0 to 4 points = 0 points

5 to 9 points = 1 point

10 to 14 points = 2 points

15 to 19 points = 3 points

20 to 24 points = 4 points

25 points or more = 5 points

Your score ___

Uneven Lie Drill 5. *Uneven Game*

A round of golf provides a number of uneven lies, and you will seldom face two similar lies in a row. To play well, you need to be able to adjust to every shot. The best way to prepare for this uncertainty is to practice a variety of lies.

For this drill, find a place where you can hit uphill, downhill, and sidehill shots to different targets. Some driving ranges have areas like this, but if you cannot find one perhaps you can find a place on the golf course itself. Take 12 balls and hit 12 different shots to 12 different targets. Pick a different target for every shot. Your goal is to put all 12 shots within 10 percent of the total distance to the target. For example, if you play from 100 yards the ball must come to rest within 10 yards of the target. Give yourself points for each swing based on the following criteria:

- Hit the ball but miss the target = 1 point each shot
- Land the ball within 20 percent of the distance to the target = 2 points each shot
- Land the ball within 10 percent of the distance to the target = 3 points each shot

Be sure to vary your shots, such as uphill lie with the ball below the feet followed by downhill lie with the ball above the feet.

To Decrease Difficulty

- Use more of the same lies and less variation.
- Increase the limit to 20 percent and 30 percent of the distance for 2 and 3 points.

To Increase Difficulty

- Vary the distance between the long clubs (3- to 5-irons) down to the wedges.
- Decrease the limit to 10 percent and 5 percent of the distance for 2 and 3 points.

Success Check

- Adjust to the slope for each lie.
- Take a practice swing before each shot to get a feel for each lie.

Score Your Success

0 to 5 points = 0 points

6 to 11 points = 1 point

12 to 17 points = 2 points

18 to 23 points = 3 points

24 to 29 points = 4 points

30 points or more = 5 points

Your score ___

STRATEGY FOR PLAYING BAD LIES

The questions of what to do and how to do it apply to bad lies as well as good lies. What shot is in front of you and what are the demands of the hole? Let's say you have a downhill lie with water between you and the green. The green is firm and surrounded by bunkers. This would be an easy shot if you were hitting from a good lie on the fairway, but with a downhill lie, it's a different story. The lie will affect the flight of the ball and your chances of getting the ball to spin so that it rotates backward in the air and stops on the green more quickly. If you still think you can get the flight necessary to stop the ball on the green, the answer to the question of how will be different than the answer for a flat fairway lie. To get the same trajectory, you will need to hit a higher-numbered club, causing the ball to fly shorter. If you still think you can make it, fire away! At other times, the only answer may be to lay up short of the water and try to make up and down from there.

The number of bad lies a golfer can face during a round are countless. Slopes and uneven lies are only a small part of what you can expect; thick rough and trees will also get in your way. Only by playing a lot of golf can you learn to deal with different lies. When asked how he knew what club to hit when he was behind a tree, Ryder Cup player Niclas Fasth answered, "Experience. There is no general rule for that because the lies will make the ball fly differently every time. I can also affect the ball flight in different ways with the same club so the answer may be different from one time to another."

A classic story in golf is Jean Van de Velde's 18th hole of the British Open at Carnoustie in 1999. He was in what looked like a safe lead as he teed off from the 18th tee. A bad drive and a bold iron shot later, he was in the creek short of the green. When he decided to take off his shoes and step into the creek to play the shot, he was really in deep trouble. It took him a triple bogey to hole out and he lost the championship to Paul Lawrie in a playoff. In retrospect, it is easy to say that Van de Velde made a couple of bad decisions and hit a couple of bad shots. Would he have made the same decisions in a smaller tournament or during an earlier round of the championship? Would he have played the shots better? Golf is about constantly considering the task at hand, weighing the risk and reward involved, and reacting to all the different lies you face.

Bad Lies Strategy Drill 1. *Mission Impossible: Long Game*

With a friend at the driving range, play a game similar to Mission Impossible in step 4 (page 51). Both of you should play from the same spot, taking turns picking the lie and the task. Visualize trees and other obstacles in your way. For example, for the first shot you might have to hit a low shot under a tree line in the back that starts right of the 100-yard marker and finishes at the 150-yard (137-meter) marker. Use 10 balls each. Score yourselves according to the following criteria:

- Wrong trajectory and miss the target = 0 points
- Accurate trajectory but way off target = 1 point
- Good trajectory and hit the target = 2 points

To Decrease Difficulty

- Use the same club but vary the targets.
- Hit two shots with the same task and see if the second one goes better.

To Increase Difficulty

- Vary targets and clubs for each shot.
- Hit from an area with rough, slopes, and other difficult lies.

Score Your Success

0 to 4 points = 1 point

5 to 8 points = 2 points

9 to 12 points = 3 points

13 to 16 points = 4 points

17 to 20 points = 5 points

Your score ___

Overcoming a Difficult Lie

Bad Lies Strategy Drill 2. *Bad Throw*

When playing a round of nine holes on the golf course with a friend, make a rule that you can throw each other's ball once on every hole. The ball cannot be thrown into a hazard and it must be possible to find and play without penalty. Play from the lie where the ball ends up. Calculate what your score would have been had your partner not thrown the ball.

To Decrease Difficulty

- Only use the throw in the short game.
- Throw the ball no more than 15 yards.

To Increase Difficulty

- Use the drill for 18 holes.
- Set no limits on where the ball can be thrown.

Success Check

- Always calculate risks and rewards when deciding what shot to play.
- Think one shot ahead of the shot at hand. From where do you want to hit your next shot?

Score Your Success

6 shots or more = 1 point

5 shots = 2 points

4 shots = 3 points

3 shots = 4 points

2 shots or fewer = 5 points

Your score ___

BAD LIE SUCCESS SUMMARY

The key to mastering bad lies is adjusting to the ground on which the ball rests. When the ball is below your feet, adjust the grip to give yourself a longer club to work with. When the ball is above your feet, shorten the club. Try to align your shoulders parallel with the ground.

When playing from an uphill or downhill lie, adjust the ball position. Move the ball forward in the stance for an uphill lie and back in the stance for a downhill lie. If you notice that good shots end up left or right of the target, keep in mind that the slope will usually cause the ball

to curve. Aim left for a downhill lie or a lie with the ball below your feet. Aim right for an uphill lie or a lie with the ball above your feet.

Record your point totals from each of the drills in this step and add them together. If you scored 21 to 35 points, you're ready for the next step. If you scored 12 to 20 points, you're almost there and can move on after reviewing the sections you feel you need to improve the most. If you scored fewer than 12 points, review the techniques and practice the drills again to raise your scores.

Uneven Lie Drills

1. Find the Ground, Uphill and Downhill Lies _____ out of 5

2. Clip the Tee, Uphill and Downhill Lies _____ out of 5

3. Find the Ground, Sidehill Lies _____ out of 5

4. Clip the Tee, Sidehill Lies _____ out of 5

5. Uneven Game _____ out of 5

Bad Lies Strategy Drills

1. Mission Impossible: Long Game _____ out of 5

2. Bad Throw _____ out of 5

Total **_____ out of 35**

The term *bad lies* may say more about the player than the actual lie itself. A lie that a new golfer would view as bad may be no problem at all to an experienced player. Becoming a better golfer is about finding more ways to execute the shots you face. If you master bad lies on the grass, you will soon be able to master the next step, bad and good lies in the bunker. Move on to the next step!

Escaping From Bunkers

Often perceived as the most difficult golf shot, the bunker shot is actually one of the easiest. With a little knowledge and practice, this shot will become a potent force in your arsenal of golf shots. Good players actually prefer playing from the sand over playing from the green-side rough because a bunker shot is easier to execute and control. In a bunker shot you hit the sand instead of the ball, sending the ball out of the bunker with the sand. Since it is easier to hit sand than a golf ball, with practice a bunker shot can become easy.

Golf course architects place bunkers in strategic locations where players are likely to hit shots.

While the white sand provides a visually pleasing contrast to the green, most players find sand bunkers more intimidating than pleasing. One of the more famous bunkers at the Old Course in St. Andrews, Scotland, has earned the name Hell Hole for the centuries of agony it has caused some players. The intimidation factor is intended to enhance the challenge and test your skill. In this step, you will learn to rise to the challenge by developing the skill to hit bunker shots from green-side and fairway bunkers.

BUNKER RULES AND ETIQUETTE

Before learning to execute bunker shots, you need to know the rules and etiquette that apply to the sand. The rule specific to bunker play is rule 13.4 of the USGA rulebook. A club is not allowed to touch the sand before the downswing motion; touching the sand results in a two-stroke penalty. Because the bunker is considered a hazard, you may not remove any natural objects such as stones, sticks, or clumps

of sand that may impede your swing or contact with the ball. However, you may remove any man-made objects such as a rake, bottles, or paper. If the ball moves as you remove a man-made object, you must replace the ball in its original position.

As a matter of etiquette, carry a rake into the bunker and place it out of your way as you set up and execute the shot. Before leaving the bunker, rake away any disturbances you created in the sand while hitting the shot or walking in the bunker (figure 7.1). Leave the bunker looking the way you would like it to look if your ball were to land there again. When leaving the bunker, place the rake with the teeth down outside or just inside the bunker.

Figure 7.1 Rake the bunker after your shot.

GREEN-SIDE BUNKER SHOTS

The sand wedge (figure 7.2) is specifically designed for use in green-side bunkers. Although the sand wedge can be effective with other shots, the heavier bottom of the club, or the bounce, makes it particularly effective in sand. Because sand is heavier than grass, the bounce allows the club to slide easily through the sand. The high loft of a sand wedge also helps you lift the ball into the air without hitting down on the ball as is required with other irons.

The bunker shot varies depending on the lie. Like other parts of the golf course, a bunker can have undulations that will affect your stance as you set up for your shot. Uneven lies (uphill, downhill, and sidehill) are common in bunkers. Stance adjustments that ensure your body is balanced and your swing follows the contours of lie as discussed in step 6 are the same in the bunker as they are in other parts of the course.

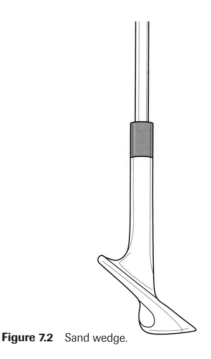

Figure 7.2 Sand wedge.

If your ball sits directly on top of the sand in a green-side bunker, you have a regular or normal lie (figure 7.3a). If the ball is plugged in the sand and resembles a fried egg, you have a buried lie (figure 7.3b). There are differences in playing shots from regular and buried lies.

Figure 7.3 Bunker lies: *(a)* regular lie; *(b)* buried lie.

Regular Lie

A green-side bunker shot is similar to a full swing except for slight modifications in the setup. To make full use of the sand wedge's bounce, open the clubface so that it points skyward and then grip the club (figure 7.4). This causes the clubface to point away from the target. To counteract the clubface's alignment, open your stance by moving the target-side foot back and adjusting the hips and shoulders to align with the feet.

To keep from sliding, shuffle your feet down into the sand an inch or two. Digging into the sand also gives you a feel for its depth and texture, which is a tip as to how the clubhead will react once it hits the sand. If the sand feels dry and fluffy, the club will slide easily. If it is damp and packed, you will need to put forth more effort to get the club through the sand. Having the feet below the ball will help you contact the sand before the ball.

To encourage the correct swing and follow-through, grip the sand wedge high on the handle as in a normal shot. Grip the handle tightly with the fingers of the left hand so that the club doesn't roll over in the sand. The shaft should point to the zipper of your pants and your hands should be slightly forward of the clubhead. Play the ball in the middle of the stance.

With the clubface open and aimed at the target, take a normal swing along the line of the shoulders, hips, and feet. Strike the sand 2 to 4 inches (5 to 10 centimeters) behind the ball, making a shallow divot about the size of a dollar bill. Let the ball splash on a blanket of sand out of the bunker and onto the green.

The key to distance control in a green-side bunker shot is the follow-through. Swing through to a complete finish for long bunker shots (up to 20 yards), but shorten the follow-through when the pin is closer. The follow-through should finish with the hips and shoulders square to the target, the body in balance, and the weight primarily on the target-side foot. It takes practice to develop a sense of touch and distance control in a bunker shot.

Figure 7.4 | A Green-Side Bunker Shot From a Regular Lie

a

b

c

SETUP

1. Open the clubface, aim toward the target, and take a normal grip

2. Grip the club firmly with the fingers of the left hand to control the club

3. Point the shaft at your zipper, hands slightly forward of the clubhead

4. Use an open stance

5. Dig your feet into the sand

EXECUTION

1. Take a normal swing along the line of the shoulders, hips, and feet

2. Strike the sand 2 to 4 inches behind the ball, taking a shallow divot of sand

3. Keep the lower body still during the swing

FOLLOW-THROUGH

1. Complete a full swing with high follow-through for long bunker shots

2. Shorten the follow-through if the hole is close to the bunker

3. Make sure the hips and shoulders are square to the target

4. Make sure you are balanced with your weight primarily on the target-side foot

Misstep

When hitting a bunker shot from a regular lie, you contact the ball instead of the sand behind the ball.

Correction

First, check your ball position to see if it's too far back in your stance. Move the ball to the middle or slightly to the target side of your stance. Second, check your downswing. You may be watching the ball rather than a spot 2 to 3 inches behind the ball. Focus on where you want the club to enter the sand on the downswing.

Misstep

When hitting a bunker shot from a regular lie, you take too much sand and the ball remains in the bunker.

Correction

First, check your ball position to see if the ball is too far forward in your stance; if it is, move the ball back to the middle of your stance. Second, check your downswing. The angle of the clubhead is probably too steep, driving the clubhead into the sand. Take a shallower swing, attempting to skim the sand out from under the ball.

Buried Lie

Playing a buried lie is similar to playing a regular lie except for a few modifications in the setup, execution, and follow-through. This shot appears even more challenging than a bunker shot from a regular lie, but like most golf shots, with a little insight and practice you'll soon hit it like a pro—it's easier than it looks.

For the setup, play the ball in the back of your stance (figure 7.5). Close the clubface so that it is turned toward the target and take a normal stance rather than an open stance. As when playing a regular lie, dig down into the sand with your feet, but place a bit more weight on the target-side foot.

On the takeaway, break the wrists a bit so that the club cocks upward. The secret to the shot is this: With the hands leading the clubhead, drive the club down behind the ball between the ball and the sand. In other words, a buried lie usually features a small space between the ball and the sand, and you should aim for this target or just behind it. Driving the clubhead into this area will cause the ball to climb up the clubface and pop out of the bunker. The sand will kill any spin on the ball, so it will come out lower and roll farther than a shot from a regular lie. If you can drive the clubhead behind the ball firmly, it will pop out and come to rest on the green.

Because you are driving the clubhead down, the sand will naturally restrict the follow-through. Your body should remain balanced throughout the shot and you should finish with the hips and shoulders angled toward the target.

Figure 7.5 — Executing a Green-Side Bunker Shot From a Buried Lie

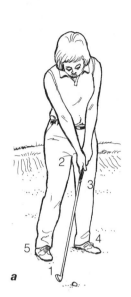

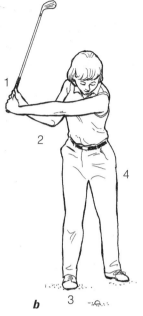

SETUP

1. Place the clubface square to the target and use a normal grip
2. Grip the club firmly with the fingers of the left hand
3. Point the shaft toward the target-side thigh, the hands ahead of the clubhead
4. Make sure your weight is on the target-side foot and the ball is in the back of the stance
5. Dig your feet into the sand

EXECUTION

1. Cock the wrist during the takeaway
2. Use a normal swing along the line of the shoulders, hips, and feet
3. Strike the sand behind the ball
4. Keep the lower body still during the swing

FOLLOW-THROUGH

1. The follow-through is abbreviated due to the club digging into the sand
2. Angle the hips and shoulders toward the target
3. Your body should be balanced with your weight primarily on the target-side foot

Misstep

When hitting a bunker shot from a buried lie, you take too much sand and the ball fails to come out of the bunker.

Correction

Check your downswing. Contact the spot just behind the ball, driving the clubhead into the sand. If your swing is too shallow, you will take too much sand.

Misstep

The ball shoots out of the bunker sideways rather than straight.

Correction

First, check your grip. If your grip is too light, the sand will move the clubhead, so you should grip the club more tightly with the three fingers on the top hand of the grip. Second, check your hand position. If the clubhead is ahead of the hands on the shot, the sand will deflect the clubhead. Keep your hands in front of the clubhead throughout the swing.

Green-Side Bunker Drill 1. *Parallel Line Progression*

Success in green-side bunker shots directly depends on your ability to move the clubhead through the sand. Striking the sand in the same place and taking a shallow, consistent divot each time helps you develop confidence and skill in making the ball fly out of the bunker and onto the green. Practice this drill to develop feel and consistency when playing out of the sand.

Draw two parallel lines in the sand approximately 4 feet long and 6 inches apart (figure 7.6). Straddle the lines as you take your setup and place the middle point between the two

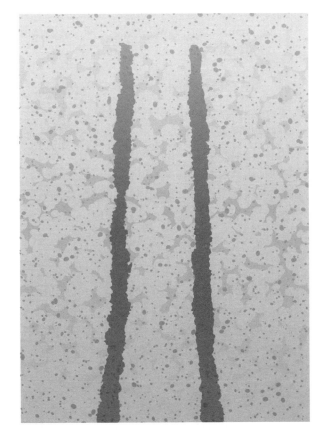

Figure 7.6 Drawing two parallel lines.

lines in the middle of your stance. Take practice swings without a ball, moving up the line after each stroke. Attempt to enter the sand on the nontarget-side line and exit the sand just before the target-side line, throwing the sand onto the green. Pay particular attention to the feel of the clubhead as it spanks the sand, taking a shallow divot. Take 5 swings. Give yourself 1 point for each swing that enters the sand on the nontarget-side line and exits just before the target-side line (5 points maximum).

Repeat the drill, placing golf balls midway between the two parallel lines. Concentrate on entering and exiting the sand, taking a shallow divot, and using the lines as a guide. Take 5 swings. Give yourself 1 point for each swing that enters and exits the sand at the lines. Give yourself 1 bonus point for each ball that reaches the green (10 points maximum).

Repeat the drill, placing golf balls just in front of and in contact with the nontarget-side line. Step on the golf balls until they are buried halfway in the sand. Focus on driving the clubhead between the line and the ball. Take 5 swings. Give yourself 1 point for each swing that enters the sand on the line just behind the ball. Give yourself 2 bonus points for each ball that reaches the green (15 points maximum).

To Decrease Difficulty

- Take half swings, concentrating on entering the sand on the back line.
- Draw a single line, straddling the line in your setup so that it is at the midpoint of your stance.
- Enter the sand on the nontarget-side of the line and exit on the target side, throwing a shallow divot of sand onto the green.

To Increase Difficulty

- Repeat all three parts of the drill using a pitching wedge and a 9-iron.
- Repeat the first part of the drill with your eyes closed.

Success Check

- For normal lies, focus on using an open clubhead and entering and exiting the sand on the lines.
- Execute a smooth, fluid swing and finish in a balanced position.
- Play the ball at the midpoint of your stance.

Score Your Success

Fewer than 5 points = 0 points

5 to 9 points = 1 point

10 to 14 points = 2 points

15 to 19 points = 3 points

20 to 24 points = 4 points

25 to 30 points = 5 points

Your score ___

Green-Side Bunker Drill 2. Rapid Fire

This drill will help you develop a natural flow in hitting bunker shots. In a bunker, place five golf balls 3 feet apart in a line running away from you and parallel to the practice green. Step up to the first ball, dig your feet into the sand, look for a target on the green, and execute the shot with a full swing. Step up to the next ball and repeat the process. Continue until you have hit all five balls. Give yourself 2 points each time you hit the green. Set up to each ball quickly and do not hesitate in executing the shot, but do not increase your swing speed. Repeat the drill three times for a total of 15 shots.

To Decrease Difficulty

- Take half swings to increase control.

To Increase Difficulty

- Alternate hitting shots from regular and buried lies.
- Choose targets at different distances for each shot.

Success Check

- Contact the sand an inch or two behind the ball so that the ball rides to the green on a blanket of sand.
- Make sure you remain balanced throughout the swing.

Score Your Success

Fewer than 5 points = 0 points

5 to 9 points = 1 point

10 to 14 points = 2 points

15 to 19 points = 3 points

20 to 24 points = 4 points

25 to 30 points = 5 points

Your score ___

Green-Side Bunker Drill 3. *Distance Control*

Place three targets on the green 5, 10, and 15 yards from the edge of the green closest to the bunker (figure 7.7). Towels, tees, or cones make good targets. Practice adjusting the length of your swing to hit bunker shots that land on or near the targets. First, hit a ball to each of the three targets, working closest to farthest. Repeat two more times for a total of nine shots. Second, repeat the entire drill with buried lies for a total of nine shots. Try to get balls to land as close to the targets as possible. Note the roll produced by each shot.

Score yourself based on the following criteria:

- Shot lands on the green = 1 point
- Shot lands one club length from the target = 2 points
- Shot hits the target on the roll = 3 points
- Shot lands on the target = 5 points

To Decrease Difficulty

- Hit shots from only good lies.
- Hit shots only to 5- and 10-yard targets.

To Increase Difficulty

- Alternate distances and lies with each shot.
- Use a pitching wedge and 9-iron and increase the target distance.
- Use different ball flight trajectories with each shot.

Success Check

- Use follow-through length to control shot distance.
- Make sure the ball comes out of the bunker on a blanket of sand.

Score Your Success

Fewer than 45 points = 0 points

45 to 59 points = 1 point

60 to 74 points = 3 points

75 to 90 points = 5 points

Your score ___

Figure 7.7 Target placement for distance control drill.

Green-Side Bunker Drill 4. *Normal-Lie Ladder*

With 11 balls, hit one ball out of the bunker from a normal lie. Hit the next shot so that it lands just beyond the last shot until you hit all 11 balls. The drill represents a ladder in that each shot is a little farther than the last. This is a good drill for working on both shot technique and distance control.

To Decrease Difficulty

- Use only six shots and hit each shot 3 to 6 feet past the last shot.

To Increase Difficulty

- Hit each shot just past and 1 yard (.9 meters) to the right or left of the last shot.

Success Check

- Keep the lower body still throughout the shot.
- Use the length of the backswing, not the speed of the swing, to control distance.

Score Your Success

Shot lands past the previous shot = 1 point each shot

Your score ____

Green-Side Bunker Drill 5. *Buried-Lie Ladder*

With 11 balls, hit one ball out of the bunker from a buried lie. Hit the next shot so that it lands just past the last shot until you hit all 11 balls. For an effective buried lie, step on the golf ball until only half of the ball is showing.

To Decrease Difficulty

- Use only six shots and hit each shot 3 to 6 feet past the last shot.

To Increase Difficulty

- Place the golf balls in uphill buried lies.
- Place the golf balls in downhill buried lies.

Success Check

- Cock the wrist on the takeaway to promote a steep descent into the sand.
- Drive the clubhead into small space between the ball and the sand.

Score Your Success

Shot lands past the previous shot = 2 points each shot

Your score ____

Green-Side Bunker Drill 6. *Uneven Lie Drill*

In a bunker, place five balls on a downhill lie, five on a level lie, and five on an uphill lie. You do not need to bury the balls for this drill. Select a landing target on the green and hit one ball from each lie to the target. Repeat until you have played all 15 balls. Give yourself 1 point for every ball that lands on the green.

Repeat the drill, placing all 15 balls in normal lies. Give yourself 1 point for every ball that lands on the green.

Repeat the drill again, placing all 15 balls in buried lies. Give yourself 1 point for every ball that lands on the green.

To Decrease Difficulty

- Select moderate slopes for uphill and downhill lies.
- Hit only the normal lies.

To Increase Difficulty

- Hit each ball to a different target.

- Increase the steepest of the slopes for uphill and downhill lies.
- Place the balls close to the lip of the bunker.

Success Check

- On uphill lies, the club should travel through the sand along the same angle as the slope.
- On downhill lies, the club should travel through the sand along the same angle as the slope.

Score Your Success

Fewer than 5 points = 0 points

6 to 15 points = 3 points

16 to 25 points = 5 points

26 to 35 points = 7 points

36 to 45 points = 10 points

Your score ___

FAIRWAY BUNKER SHOTS

Golf course designers often place fairway bunkers where tee shots or layup shots are likely to land, thus increasing the difficulty of the course. Because a fairway bunker shot (figure 7.8) requires you to hit the ball so that it travels accurately for some distance, you need to make solid contact with the club. Unlike the green-side bunker shot, the fairway bunker shot requires the clubhead to directly meet the ball. To promote this contact, you will need to make several adjustments to the setup and execution of the shot.

Dig down into the sand with your feet when taking your stance. This gives you a feel for the firmness of the sand, but more importantly it stabilizes your lower body. A stable body makes it much easier to bring the clubhead directly back to the ball. Your weight should be evenly distributed between both feet.

A key factor in this shot is striking the ball before the sand, so ball position in the setup is crucial. The sand will slow the clubhead speed and potentially misdirect the shot. You can use any club, from a fairway metal to a sand wedge, for this shot. (See the strategy section beginning on page 75 for more information on club selection.) For setup purposes, the club and lie determine ball position. If you choose a fairway metal, the ball should be just to the target side of the center. As shaft length decreases with the irons, progressively move the ball back in your stance. For example, play the ball just in front of your nontarget-side foot if you are using a pitching wedge.

If you have an uphill lie, play the ball farther up in your stance (closer to your target-side foot). If you have a downhill lie, play the ball a little closer to your nontarget-side foot. When playing from an uphill or downhill lie, your hips and shoulders should be parallel with the slope of the bunker and your weight should be as evenly distributed between both feet as possible. Again, these adjustments will give you the best chance of making clean contact with the ball.

The fairway bunker shot should not be rushed. Because most golfers have a bit of fear when executing a fairway bunker shot, they tend to rush the shot and overswing. Be aware of this tendency and calm yourself before taking the shot. Control is more important than power because solid ball contact is the key to this shot. Stand tall to the ball to ensure clean contact. Loosen your grip to promote a smooth, controlled swing. Be careful to keep the clubhead above the sand, as touching your club to the ground in a hazard is a two-stroke penalty (rule 13.4).

To promote a shallow angle into the ball, keep the takeaway low and slow. The clubhead, hands, arms, and shoulders move away from the ball in one piece, just as they do in a normal full swing. The lower body remains set—there is no weight transfer. The less the lower body moves, the greater the chance the clubhead will return directly to the ball. On the downswing, focus on the front of the ball. This will help you get the clubhead through the ball before you contact any sand.

The follow-through is the same as in the full swing. The clubhead fully extends through the ball, weight is naturally carried onto the target side of the body, and the nontarget shoulder drives under and past the chin. The body finishes in balance.

Figure 7.8   Executing a Fairway Bunker Shot

SETUP

1. Dig your feet into the sand
2. Use a light grip to promote a relaxed, controlled swing
3. Use a normal stance, evenly distributing weight between both feet
4. Position the ball in the middle to back of the stance for a normal lie
5. Keep the clubhead above the sand

EXECUTION

1. Use a normal swing along the line of the shoulders, hips, and feet
2. Strike the ball cleanly, attempting to sweep the ball off the sand
3. Keep the lower body still during the swing

FOLLOW-THROUGH

1. Complete the full swing with high follow-through for long bunker shots
2. Weight should move naturally to the target side of the body
3. Keep the body balanced throughout the swing

Misstep

You strike the sand before hitting the ball.

Correction

Check your ball position, weight distribution, and grip. If the ball is too far forward, you will have difficulty getting the club on the ball before hitting the sand, so move the ball back in your stance. If you have more weight on your rear foot during the downswing, the club will strike the sand first, so evenly distribute the weight between both feet. A tight grip will produce tension, making it difficult to hit through the ball, so relax your grip, particularly your fingers.

Fairway Bunker Drill 1. *Progressive Clubs*

From a practice fairway bunker, stroke five balls with a 9-iron, five with a 7-iron, and five with a high-lofted fairway metal (5-, 7-, or 9-metal). The point of the drill is to make clean contact with the ball before hitting the sand. Do not use a target for this drill; simply concentrate on making solid ball contact.

Score yourself based on the following criteria:

- When using the 9-iron, the ball clears the bunker = 1 point
- When using the 9-iron, the ball clears the bunker and travels 50 yards (46 meters) or more = 2 points
- When using the 7-iron, the ball clears the bunker = 1 point
- When using the 7-iron, the ball clears the bunker and travels 75 yards (69 meters) or more = 2 points
- When using the high-lofted fairway metal, the ball clears the bunker = 1 point
- When using the high-lofted fairway metal, the ball clears the bunker and travels 100 yards (91 meters) or more = 2 points

To Decrease Difficulty

- Use a pitching wedge, 9-iron, and 8-iron for the drill. It is easier to make ball contact with a higher-lofted club.

- Use half shots. Swing back to a 3-o'clock position, then downswing to a 9-o'clock position.

To Increase Difficulty

- Play from a medium- or high-lipped bunker.
- Use a 5-iron, 3-iron, and 3-metal for the drill.

Success Check

- Swing with the shoulders as the lower body remains quiet.
- Play the ball back in the stance.
- Dig your feet an inch or two into the sand.

Score Your Success

Fewer than 10 points = 0 points

10 to 14 points = 3 points

15 to 19 points = 5 points

20 to 24 points = 7 points

25 to 30 points = 10 points

Your score ___

Fairway Bunker Drill 2. *Lie Drill*

In a practice fairway bunker using a 9-iron, stroke five balls from a level lie, five from a downhill lie, five from an uphill lie, five from a sidehill lie with the ball above your feet, and five from a sidehill lie with the ball below your feet, taking 25 total shots.

Score yourself based on the following criteria:

- Contact the ball before the sand, ball remains in the bunker = 1 point
- Contact the ball before the sand, ball lands outside the bunker = 2 points
- Contact the ball before the sand, ball lands at least 10 yards outside the bunker = 3 points

To Decrease Difficulty

- Use a pitching wedge.
- Use half shots. Swing back to a 3-o'clock position, then downswing to a 9-o'clock position.

To Increase Difficulty

- Use a 4-iron or fairway metal.
- Play from a medium- or high-lipped bunker.

Success Check

- Keep the lower body still throughout the swing.
- Generate power for the shot with the shoulder turn.
- Stroke should be controlled and smooth rather than rushed and quick.

Score Your Success

Fewer than 25 points = 0 points

25 to 34 points = 2 points

35 to 44 points = 4 points

45 to 54 points = 6 points

55 to 64 points = 8 points

65 to 75 points = 10 points

Your score ___

BUNKER PLAY STRATEGY

The first strategic decision when playing a green-side bunker shot is to determine the target landing spot. Consider the lie when making this decision. A normal lie will permit you to land the ball on the green with moderate roll, while a shot from a buried lie will cause the ball to roll more. Consider where you want the ball to land so that it will roll near or perhaps even into the hole. The tighter you focus on your target, the greater the chance you have of hitting it.

The first strategic decision when playing a ball from a fairway bunker is to determine which club will allow you to clear the lip of the bunker. Some fairway bunkers, like those at the Old Course in St. Andrews, have very steep walls. In these situations, a high-lofted club or sand wedge are the only options for escaping the bunker. Even then, the ball has to be played out sideways or backward if there is to be any hope of finding the fairway. Getting out of the bunker is the first priority. Do not be too greedy. Select a club that you are confident will get the ball in the air high enough to clear the bunker.

Misstep

The ball hits the side of the bunker.

Correction

If the club has insufficient loft, the ball will not fly high enough to clear the bunker. Choose a club that you are confident will safely clear the bunker.

The second strategic decision when playing a ball from a fairway bunker is distance. Do you have a reasonable chance of reaching the green from the bunker or will you need to hit a layup shot? In either case, you need to select the club that will allow you to put the ball in your target area. Because a fairway bunker shot demands a smooth, controlled swing rather than power, select a slightly stronger club than you would ordinarily use. For example, if the green is 140 yards (128 meters) away and your normal 140-yard club is a 7-iron, consider using a 6-iron if a 6-iron will safely clear the bunker lip.

Misstep

The ball lands short of the target.

Correction

The fairway bunker shot requires a smooth, relaxed swing to ensure solid contact. Take one more club than normal for the desired distance.

BUNKER SHOT SUCCESS SUMMARY

Shots played from the bunker need not be difficult. Just remember to assess the lie (normal, uneven, or buried), plan the appropriate shot for the lie and distance (green-side or fairway bunker), and make the appropriate modifications to your setup and swing. Review the points in figures 7.4, 7.5, and 7.8 to be sure you are developing the appropriate technique for these shots. Practice the drills to refine your skills and gain the confidence necessary to successfully play these shots on the course.

Record your point totals from each of the drills in this step and add them together. If you scored at least 50 out of 75 points, you're ready for the next step. If you scored at least 35 points but fewer than 50, you are almost there. Move on after reviewing the sections that you feel you need to improve the most. If you scored fewer than 35 points, review the techniques and practice the drills again to raise your scores before moving on to the next step.

Green-Side Bunker Drills

1. Parallel Line Progression   ___ out of 5

2. Rapid Fire   ___ out of 5

3. Distance Control   ___ out of 5

4. Normal-Lie Ladder   ___ out of 10

5. Buried-Lie Ladder   ___ out of 20

6. Uneven Lie Drill   ___ out of 10

Fairway Bunker Drills

1. Progressive Clubs   ___ out of 10

2. Lie Drill   ___ out of 10

Total   ___ **out of 75**

Gary Player, one of the few individuals to win all four of golf's major championships (British Open, U.S. Open, Masters, and PGA Championship) had this to say about escaping from bunkers: "No bunker shot has ever scared me, and none ever will. The key to this bravado is practice. There are no shortcuts; you must practice." The point is that escaping from bunkers is not a matter of luck, it is a matter of practice. In this step, you have learned and practiced the fundamentals of effective bunker play. Continued practice is synonymous with continued improvement in bunker play.

While few players intend to put their ball in the bunker, it eventually finds its way there if you play enough golf. Being prepared to play the shot you get will keep you in the game. We follow this theme into the next step, playing shots from places the ball wasn't intended to go. We will review the fundamentals of making shots when your ball misses the fairway or green and you find yourself looking to hit the ball from the tall grass or rough. Again, these shots are challenging, but with a little knowledge and a fair amount of practice, they can be made with success. Take your next step to success in golf by learning step 8, Hitting Shots From the Rough.

Hitting Shots From the Rough

Ideally every shot would hit the fairway or green, but this just isn't going to happen, and on occasion you will find your ball in the rough. Even the best players in the game miss a fairway or green and must play from the rough. One of the reasons these players are great is, they know the techniques for hitting successful shots under conditions that are less than ideal.

When a golf course superintendent, the person in charge of the course setup and maintenance, wants to make the course more challenging or difficult, one way to do this is known as growing the rough. Because the quality of both golfers and golf equipment has improved over the years, tournament directors and course superintendents often look for ways to make courses more challenging. One of the fastest and least expensive ways of doing this is to grow the rough. This means players will see more rough on more courses as time goes on.

The rough can be grown in two ways. First, the superintendent can mow less of the fairway, increasing the amount of tall grass defining the sides and both ends of the fairway. This is known as narrowing the fairway.

A second way of growing the rough is letting the grass along the fairway grow taller so that there are different levels of rough. For example, a superintendent may let the first 3 or 4 yards (2.7 to 3.7 meters) of grass on the sides of a fairway grow an inch or two taller than the fairway. This is known as the first cut of rough. After 3 or 4 yards, the grass may be grown to 4 to 6 inches (10 to 15 centimeters). This is known as the second cut of rough. In some circumstances, there may be a third cut of rough in which the grass is not cut at all. Depending on the type of grass, you may find yourself looking for your ball in grass that is knee- or even waist-high. When setting up a golf course for the U.S. Open, the USGA is notorious for growing the rough so as to make the course incredibly difficult. The rough is a fact of life on a golf course, and to be a successful golfer you must learn to play from it.

SHOOTING FROM THE ROUGH

A shot from the rough (figure 8.1) is hit like a normal shot, with two adjustments. These adjustments apply whether you are attempting a full swing from fairway rough or a partial swing pitch shot from green-side rough.

First, as you take your stance and address the ball, open the clubface slightly. Tall grass has a tendency to catch the club around the hosel, twisting the clubface shut and sending the shot left for a right-handed player or right for a left-handed player. Opening the clubface slightly at address compensates for this.

Second, during the takeaway break your wrists slightly so that you take the club up more abruptly. The tall grass will slow the clubhead down before it reaches the ball, so you must get as much clubhead on the ball while catching as little grass as possible on the downswing. Lifting

Figure 8.1 — Executing a Shot From the Rough

PREPARATION

1. Open the clubface at address
2. Play the ball back in the stance
3. Use a firm grip

TAKEAWAY

1. Early in the takeaway, break the wrists and bring the club up at a steep angle
2. The arms, hands, and club should naturally follow the turn of the shoulders
3. The hips and legs should turn naturally in response to the turn of the shoulders

Misstep

You hit behind the ball, catching more grass than ball.

Correction

You aren't using a steep angle of descent. Break the wrists on the takeaway to abruptly lift the club. On the downswing, pull down on the handle to maintain an up-and-down steep angle of descent into the ball. Shift your weight. Make sure your weight is forward on the target-side foot when you make contact.

the clubhead abruptly on the takeaway allows you to bring the head back to the ball at a steeper angle and minimizes the amount of grass you catch before contacting the ball. Playing the ball slightly back in your stance, particularly on shots from green-side rough, will also help you make cleaner contact with the ball.

If you are playing the ball from moderate to deep rough, tighten your grip a bit. This will help minimize the effect the grass has on your golf club. If you are pitching the ball less than 50 yards to a green, open the clubface and swing about 50 percent harder than you think is necessary. The clubhead will slide under the ball and pop it out. If you are chipping the ball onto the green from deep rough, exaggerate the wrist break on the takeaway and be aggressive on the downswing to get the clubhead through the grass. For shorter shots, take a shorter back-swing. You must hit these shots aggressively to get the clubhead through the tall grass.

DOWNSWING	FOLLOW-THROUGH

DOWNSWING

1. Shift your weight from the back to the front foot
2. Pull down sharply on the club handle to maintain a steep angle of descent into the ball
3. Build shot speed slowly to accelerate down and through the rough to the ball
4. Attempt to minimize contact with the grass and maximize contact with the ball

FOLLOW-THROUGH

1. The club should follow the ball toward the target
2. Finish on balance with your weight on the target-side foot

Misstep

The ball is pulled off the target line.

Correction

Maintain an open clubface. Tall grass grabs the hosel of the club and shuts the clubface, so you need to compensate by opening the clubface at address and maintaining a firm grip.

Shot From the Rough Drill 1. *Angle of Attack*

To successfully play a shot from the rough, you must bring the clubhead into the ball with a steep angle of attack, taking a minimal amount of grass as you swing. This drill will help you develop a steeper angle of descent. You do not need to hit shots from the rough for this drill.

On a driving range, place a board or other object one yard behind a golf ball (figure 8.2). Using a 9-iron or pitching wedge, assume a normal stance with the ball in the middle of the stance. Begin the takeaway by breaking your wrists and lifting the clubhead straight back and directly into the air over the board. Repeat 10 times. Give yourself 1 point every time you clear the board on your takeaway.

Repeat the drill, only this time complete your backswing. Repeat 10 times. Give yourself 1 point every time you clear the board on your takeaway and backswing.

Finally, repeat the drill, executing the takeaway and backswing, completing the swing, and striking the ball. On the downswing, pull the handle of the club down sharply to maintain a steep angle of descent into the ball. The swing should feel controlled and contact with the ball should be crisp. Repeat 10 times. Give yourself 1 point for clearing the board on your takeaway and backswing and 1 point for crisp contact with the ball (strike the ball before the ground).

To Decrease Difficulty

- Hit three-quarter swing shots rather than full swing shots.

To Increase Difficulty

- Execute the drill using a wedge, iron, and fairway metal.

Success Check

- Begin the backswing by lifting the club abruptly and breaking the wrists.
- Maintain a steep angle of descent throughout the shot.
- Execute the shot in a relaxed, rhythmic manner.

Score Your Success

1 to 9 points = 5 points

10 to 19 points = 10 points

20 to 29 points = 15 points

30 to 40 points = 20 points

Your score ___

Figure 8.2 Angle of attack drill.

Shot From the Rough Drill 2. *In the Rough*

To become familiar with playing the ball out of the rough, you may have to do some searching to find a place where you can practice taking partial or full swings at a ball.

From medium rough (2 to 4 inches), chip a golf ball to a target. Emphasize a steep angle of attack, maximum contact with the ball, and minimum contact with the grass. The chip should be no more than a three-quarter swing. Hit 15 chip shots, 5 to a target 10 yards away, 5 to a target 15 yards away, and 5 to a target 20 yards away. Give yourself 2 points for every chip shot that travels at least 5 yards in the air.

Now, from medium rough pitch a golf ball to a target, this time using a full swing with an emphasis on lifting the club abruptly on the takeaway and striking the ball using a steep angle of attack. Hit five pitch shots to a target 25 yards (23 meters) away, five pitch shots to a target 35 yards (32 meters) away, and five pitch shots to a target 45 yards (41 meters) away. Give yourself 2 points for each pitch shot that travels at least 10 yards in the air and 5 points for each pitch shot that travels at least 20 yards.

To Decrease Difficulty

- Hit shots from light rough.

To Increase Difficulty

- Hit shots from rough where only the very top of the ball is visible.
- Change the depth of rough with each shot.

Success Check

- Maintain a firm grip throughout the swing.
- Keep the clubface open at address.
- Execute the shot in a relaxed, rhythmic manner.

Score Your Success

0 to 49 points = 0 points

50 to 59 points = 2 points

60 to 69 points = 4 points

70 to 79 points = 6 points

80 to 89 points = 8 points

90 to 105 points = 10 points

Your score ___

Shot From the Rough Drill 3. *Short but Deadly Shots*

When a golf ball is surrounded or partially covered by grass, it is difficult to get the clubhead cleanly on the ball, which makes the shot difficult to control. This can be a particular problem when the rough is around the green and the shot requires a bit of touch to get it close to the hole. From a lie in medium rough (no higher than the tops of your shoes), chip a golf ball to a hole that is fewer than 10 yards away. Repeat 10 times.

To Decrease Difficulty

- Hit shots from light rough (midway up your shoes).
- Hit shots to a hole that is 20 to 30 yards away. The more green you have to work with, the easier the shots are as the ball has a tendency to roll more when coming out of the rough.

To Increase Difficulty

- Execute the drill from rough where only the very top of the ball is visible.

Success Check

- Bring the clubhead up sharply at takeaway.
- Use a steep angle of descent to contact more of the ball and less of the grass.

Score Your Success

Ball lands on the green = 1 point

Ball stops within 3 feet of hole = 2 points

Your score ___

Shot From the Rough Drill 4. _Pitching From the Rough_

From a lie in medium rough (no higher than the tops of your shoes), use a sand wedge to pitch a golf ball to a hole on a green that is 20 to 30 yards away. Repeat 10 times. Remember to open the clubface and swing aggressively. The ball will roll more because it will have less spin coming out of the rough.

To Decrease Difficulty

- Hit shots from light rough (midway up your shoes).

To Increase Difficulty

- Aim for a hole within 5 yards of the edge of the green nearest to you.
- Execute the shot so that the ball must carry a sand bunker before landing on the green.

Success Check

- Make sure the clubface remains open.
- Swing aggressively.
- Use a firm grip with the left hand to keep the club from turning in the tall grass.
- Keep the body balanced throughout the swing.

Score Your Success

Ball lands on the green = 2 points

Ball stops within 3 feet of the hole = 3 points

Your score ___

ROUGH PLAY STRATEGY

Playing from the rough is a bit more complicated than playing from the fairway, and some strategic thinking is necessary to carry off the shot. In this section, we will cover the major strategy points and offer some suggestions for making the best of a difficult situation.

First, ask yourself what sort of grass you are in. Is the grass thick or sparse? How high is it? Is the ball sitting down or up in the grass or somewhere in between? How far do you have to hit the ball to get it back to the fairway or onto the green? When playing from a difficult lie, the first consideration is getting the ball back into reasonable play. In golf, the conservative strategy is generally the smarter strategy. Do not make a bad situation worse—play safe and don't be greedy.

Once you know what sort of grass you are playing from, decide what shot you want to hit. For example, if the ball is 180 yards (165 meters) from the green and buried so that little of the ball is showing, you will have to dig deep into the rough to extract the ball (figure 8.3).

With so much grass covering the ball, there is slim hope that you will reach the green, so you may decide simply to advance the ball 30 yards back onto the fairway. If the ball is sitting up on thick green-side rough 3 yards from the green, you should have no problem contacting the ball cleanly with minimal interference from the grass (figure 8.4), so you might decide to attempt to hole the ball with a chip shot.

Figure 8.3 If the ball is deeply buried in the rough, your goal should be to get the ball back onto the fairway.

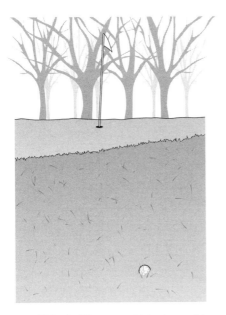

Figure 8.4 If the ball is up on thick green-side rough, try to get the ball in the hole with a chip shot.

Once you decide what shot you want to take, you need to select a club that will let you execute the shot. Because the clubhead will likely catch the grass first and then the ball, the rough will slow the clubhead down and influence its direction in unpredictable ways. It is necessary to select a club that will minimize the effect of the rough on your shot. For average golfers, a 5-iron is the club with the least loft that they can effectively play from any rough (figure 8.5). If using a fairway wood, a 5-wood is about the limit of

effective loft. Any less loft and you will have difficulty getting the clubhead to make reasonable contact with the ball.

If the ball is sitting in light or moderate rough, neither perched nor buried and with most of the ball showing, it is in a flyer lie (figure 8.6). When a ball is in a flyer lie, the clubhead will make contact with the grass before the ball. The grass will not reduce clubhead speed because it is not very thick, but some grass will come between the clubhead and the ball, reducing the backspin on the ball so that the shot is virtually spinless. The ball will come out faster, fly lower, and bounce and run longer. A ball struck well from a flyer lie will roll a long way. When hitting from a flyer lie, take one less club than you normally would in order to account for the greater ball roll. For example, if you normally hit a 7-iron 140 yards, take an 8-iron for the same distance with a flyer lie.

Figure 8.6 Flyer lie.

When the ball is buried in heavy rough, your goal is to simply get the ball out and back to the short grass (figure 8.7). Don't run up your score by trying for too much distance. Given the amount of grass the clubhead must fight through to reach the ball, you are not likely to make contact that is sufficient enough to gain much length. A wedge is usually a good choice. Play

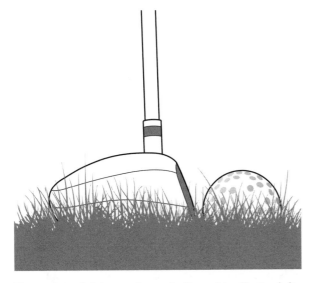

Figure 8.5 A 5-iron or 5-wood will provide effective loft for hitting a shot from the rough.

Figure 8.7 Ball buried in heavy rough.

the ball back in your stance, break your wrists on the takeaway, and use a steep up-and-down swing to extract the ball. A general rule of thumb is the deeper the lie, the steeper the descent.

When most golfers find their ball perched on top of thick rough (figure 8.8), they consider themselves lucky. But they shouldn't think they've got an easy shot. It isn't hard to whiff this shot or pop the ball straight in the air by getting the clubhead too far under the ball. This shot should be hit more like a tee shot—a low, driving shot rather than a steep, downward approach. In other words, it is the opposite of the shot for a ball buried in heavy rough. Select a club that will send the ball the required distance, as no grass should inhibit this shot. To promote the shallow, sweeping action needed for this shot, take the club back long and low.

Figure 8.8   Hitting a ball perched on top of heavy rough.

Strategic Play
From the Rough Drill 1.   *High, Medium, or Low*

Using a practice green with deep rough within 20 yards, place 10 balls deep into the rough (step on them, figure 8.9a), 10 balls at a medium distance in the rough (drop them from shoulder- or hip-height, figure 8.9b), and 10 balls perched on top of the rough (place them gently on the grass, figure 8.9c). Pick a target in the middle of the green 15 to

20 yards away and pitch the 30 balls to this target. For each of the three lies, find the club that gets the ball consistently closest to the target. For each shot, give yourself 2 points if the ball lands on the green and an additional 3 points if the ball stops within 5 yards of the target hole.

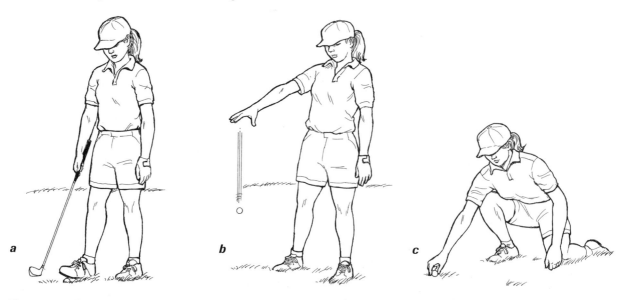

Figure 8.9   Ball setup for the high, medium, or low drill: *(a)* put balls deep in the rough by stepping on them; *(b)* put balls at a medium level in the rough by dropping them from shoulder or hip height; *(c)* put balls on top of the rough by carefully placing them.

To Decrease Difficulty

- Play five balls from each lie and place the balls within 10 yards of the practice green.

To Increase Difficulty

- Vary the distance to the green for each of the 10 balls in the three lies.

Success Check

- Adjust the angle of the clubhead descent for each particular lie.

Score Your Success

74 points or fewer = 0 points

75 to 89 points = 2 points

90 to 104 points = 4 points

105 to 119 points = 6 points

120 to 134 points = 8 points

135 to 150 points = 10 points

Your score ___

Strategic Play From the Rough Drill 2. *Perched Shot*

Perch 10 balls on top of thick rough approximately 20 yards from the practice green. Using a sand wedge, alternate pitching the balls to two holes at different distances on the practice green. Repeat.

Score yourself based on the following criteria:

- Ball lands and remains on the green = 1 point
- Ball comes to rest within 6 feet of the hole = 2 points
- Ball comes to rest within 3 feet of the hole = 3 points

To Decrease Difficulty

- Play shots 10 yards from the practice green.
- Play shots to the same hole.

To Increase Difficulty

- Vary the distance to the green for each shot.
- Play each shot to a different hole.

Success Check

- Take the club back long and low to promote a shallow, sweeping action.

Score Your Success

29 points or fewer = 0 points

30 to 39 points = 1 point

40 to 49 points = 3 points

50 to 60 points = 5 points

Your score ___

ROUGH SHOTS SUCCESS SUMMARY

Knowing how to play the ball from the rough will give you a major advantage over your opponents and the golf course. With a few simple adjustments to your swing and a reduction in your expectations for the shot, you will minimize the chances of finding your ball in the rough. Make no mistake: Playing from the rough is tough, but it is a reality for every golfer, even the greatest. Players who practice these shots and think strategically will feel less frustration when they find their balls in the rough because they will know how to get out of trouble.

Record your point totals from each of the drills in this step and add them together. If you scored at least 80 out of 95 points, you're ready for the next step. If you scored at least 60 points but fewer than 80, you are almost there. Move on after reviewing the sections where you need the most improvement. If you scored fewer than 60 points, review the techniques and practice the drills again to raise your scores.

Shot From the Rough Drills

1. Angle of Attack   ___ out of 20

2. In the Rough   ___ out of 10

3. Short but Deadly Shots   ___ out of 20

4. Pitching From the Rough   ___ out of 30

Strategic Play From the Rough Drills

1. High, Medium, or Low   ___ out of 10

2. Perched Shot   ___ out of 5

Total   ___ *out of 95*

Some of the most challenging shots in golf come from the rough. Now that you know and have practiced the techniques and strategies for dealing with these difficult shots, you can deal effectively with most of the trouble a golf course may present. Steps 1 through 8 have focused primarily on skills and shots that help you move your ball successfully around a golf course. The next series of steps builds on your golfing skills by offering information that will help you make appropriate decisions on the golf course. Good decisions are as much a part of success as shot-making skills. We begin in step 9 with selecting the right club.

Selecting the Right Club

Once you have learned how to get the ball in the air, you will start noticing differences between clubs. According to the rules of golf, a player is allowed to carry 14 clubs; which 14 clubs he or she decides to carry is totally up to the player. Good players usually carry the same clubs each week, but they also have a few clubs they change depending on the characteristics of the golf course. A specific course may lead a golfer to add an extra wedge, an extra long iron such as a 1- or 2-iron, or an extra wood such as a 5- or 7-wood. High-caliber players know it pays off to spend some time finding the mix of clubs that will allow them to play the shots that the course requires. A new golfer's challenge when mastering club selection is to understand the ways different clubs affect the ball.

For a new golfer it may seem a bit much to carry 14 clubs. It is a good idea to start out with a short set of two woods, four or five irons, and a putter. Still, it is important to find out as soon as possible what the different clubs do to the ball so that you can understand the reasoning behind carrying 14 clubs.

A general rule is, the lower the number of the club, the lower the trajectory and the longer the ball will travel in the air. This concept applies to irons as well as woods. Wedges give the ball the highest trajectory and shortest flight as well as the most spin, which causes the ball to stop quickly as it lands. As you move to lower-numbered irons, ball flight will be lower and longer and the ball will spin less. A 5- or 7-wood can replace the lowest-numbered irons since the woods are usually easier to use. (LPGA player Carin Koch says ladies should not carry irons lower than 4 or 5 and can instead complete their sets of clubs with a 7-, 9-, or 11-wood.)As you move to lower-numbered woods down to the driver (1), the ball will travel farther. The driver is used mostly off the tee box but good players can also use it from the fairway if the lie is good and they want to hit the ball as far as possible.

As you progress it is important to learn how far you hit each club in your bag. See step 10 for more details.

CLUB SELECTION

The actual club selection is done during the preparation phase for the shot. While preparing for the shot, stand behind the ball and gather as much information as possible. Check the wind and determine the lie of the ball. Are you playing in dry or wet conditions? What is the landing area like? To choose the right club, you need to consider the circumstances.

If you are playing into the wind, the ball will lose distance and you will need to play a longer club than you would without the wind. If you are playing with the wind, the wind will help the ball and you will need to select a shorter club.

The lie will affect the distance of the ball as well. When the ball is in thick grass, the shot will be shorter since the grass will lower the clubhead speed. This condition could also cause a so-called flyer, which even good players sometimes have problems with. Grass between the ball and the club decreases the spin on the ball, causing it to fly longer.

How to hit a ball in a bare lie depends on how well you feel you can hit the ball. Generally a bare lie should not be a problem since you will want to hit the ball on the downswing. A slight mishit will cause the ball to go shorter than normal.

When hitting a downhill lie, try to keep the same clubhead speed as in a normal lie so that the ball will come out lower and travel farther in the air. It probably will be difficult to maintain clubhead speed, however, so the ball will go shorter. An uphill lie will increase the loft on the club and the ball will travel higher and shorter than from a normal lie. Because of lost clubhead speed, a sidehill lie will probably cause the ball to travel shorter.

Club selection is not only about picking a certain club. Variations in the way the ball travels can be created in more than one way, and good players have numerous ways to use every club in the bag. One of the first British instructors to go to Sweden was a man named John Cockin. He later became a highly respected chairman of the Swedish PGA. Cockin said, "Think of a golfer as a table tennis player. A table tennis player only has one racket but think of the number of different shots he can hit with that racket. If a

golfer can come anywhere close to that number of ways to use each one of his or her clubs there is enough to work on for a life in golf."

A good player is not stuck with only one way to swing a club. Depending on the circumstances (lie, wind, target, and so on), there are many variations for using the same club. Start on the driving range by hitting to a target with each club. Try to find out what modifications you need to get the ball to fly as you would like it to. What happens if you grip down on the club, if you swing slower or shorter, or if you move the ball back in your stance or forward? Finding out the effects of small or large alterations in setup, grip, and swing is a great way of practicing. Experiment with modifications on the driving range as well as on the course.

Iron Club Selection

The irons in a player's bag can range from a 1- or 2-iron to a 9-iron and a few wedges. A pitching wedge of 48 degrees, a gap wedge of 52 degrees, a sand wedge of 56 degrees, and a lob wedge of 60 degrees are some of the different options. Good players generally try to pick three or four wedges to eliminate gaps between clubs (distances for which they have no club to hit a comfortable shot with).

Irons are used anywhere from very close to the green for chipping or pitching (see step 3 and step 4 for ideas on choosing clubs for chipping and pitching) to off a tee on a par-3 hole, or any hole where you need more control than a wood provides. When selecting an iron (figure 9.1), consider the following factors:

- Lie—Will it cause the ball to go longer or shorter?

- Weather and wind—Will it cause the ball to go longer or shorter?

- Area where the ball will land—Do you need to put a lot of spin on the ball or do you want the ball to run when it lands?

- Trajectory—Is a high or a low shot more favorable?

- Ball flight—Is there any need to curve the ball right or left?

With these factors in mind, you can make a decision based on the numbers on the clubs. A lower-numbered club will cause the ball to go longer and lower than a higher-numbered club. A higher-numbered club will give the ball more spin and cause it to stop on the green more quickly, both because of spin and the height of the shot. A lower-numbered club will be easier to use if you need to give the ball sidespin.

Figure 9.1   Selecting an Iron Club

1. The lower the club number, the farther the ball will fly
2. The lower the club number, the lower the trajectory
3. The lower the club number, the more difficult it will be to control the shot since sidespin increases with lower numbers
4. The lower the club number, the closer the ball should be positioned to the left heel

Misstep

You try to help the ball get up in the air, causing you to top the ball.

Correction

When the club reaches the ball, it has already reached its lowest point. The golf swing is a downward movement, so only the loft of the club should help the ball up in the air. Hit down on the ball.

Misstep

You end up short of the target.

Correction

The ball's flight will be short if you slightly miss the center of the clubface. Hitting the toe or heel of the club will cause the ball to go shorter and it may also cause the ball to go sideways. Always take one extra club so that even if you mishit the ball you will still reach your target.

Iron Club Drill 1. *The Stepladder*

Use the same swing tempo and hit four balls each with a 9- or 8-iron, 6- or 5-iron, and 4- or 3-iron, for a total of 12 shots. Select three targets you think you can reach with the different shots. Alternate targets and clubs between shots. Give yourself points based on the following criteria:

- Mishit the ball so that it does not fly the way it should = 0 points
- Make solid contact with the ball, ball ends up nowhere near the target = 1 point
- Make solid contact with the ball, ball ends up somewhere around the target = 2 points
- Hit a good shot, ball ends up at the target = 3 points

To Decrease Difficulty

- Hit all shots with the same club before you change club and target.
- Use a wedge, 9-iron, and 8-iron or other clubs close to each other.

To Increase Difficulty

- Hit only one shot with the same club and then change both club and target.
- Use a middle iron, a long iron, and a wood.

Success Check

- Take a normal swing and keep your focus on the target.
- Try to keep the same tempo with all clubs.

Score Your Success

0 to 4 points = 0 points

5 to 9 points = 1 point

10 to 14 points = 2 points

15 to 21 points = 3 points

22 to 27 points = 4 points

28 points or more = 5 points

Your score ____

Iron Club Drill 2. *The Triple*

With a 7- or 8-iron, hit three balls to a 100-yard (91-meter) target, three balls to a 125-yard (114-meter) target, and three balls to a 150-yard (137-meter) target. If the distance is too far, choose three other distances as long as they allow you to play a shorter shot than normal, a normal shot, and a longer shot than normal with the selected club. After you have hit nine balls, work backward, starting with three shots to the 150-yard target, three to the 125-yard target, and three to the 100-yard target. Give yourself 1 point every time you hit the right distance or the right direction and give yourself 2 points every time you hit the right distance and direction. Try to hit at least two shots out of three at each distance with the right distance and direction.

To Decrease Difficulty

- Start with a wedge and closer targets.

- Use only two distances, one normal and one shorter than normal, and hit four balls to each target.

To Increase Difficulty

- Use a club that will prevent you from hitting a normal shot to the target. Pick three targets that are all shorter or all longer than you would normally hit with the club you selected.
- Play only one shot to a target before you move to the next target.

Success Check

- Adjust your tempo to change the distance the ball flies.
- See what happens when you grip farther down the shaft of the club.

Score Your Success

0 to 4 points = 0 points

5 to 9 points = 1 point

10 to 14 points = 2 points

15 to 21 points = 3 points

22 to 27 points = 4 points

28 points or more = 5 points

Your score ___

Iron Club Drill 3. *Alteration Drill*

Use a 6-, 7-, or 8-iron for each shot in this drill. Make the alterations shown in figure 9.2 and play four shots with each alteration, using the same club on all shots. Note what happens to the ball in terms of trajectory (lower, higher, shorter, longer).

To Decrease Difficulty

- Start by using only two of the alterations (for example, ball forward or back in stance).
- Use a shorter iron.

To Increase Difficulty

- Use a different club for each shot and score yourself compared to the normal trajectory for that club.
- Use a longer iron.

Success Check

- Make your normal preparations for each shot and take aim at a target for every shot.
- Concentrate on the alteration you are about to make and letting the ball react to your swing.

Score Your Success

Two shots with the same alteration give the same result = 1 point

Three shots with the same alteration give the same result = 3 points

All four shots with the same alteration give the same result = 5 points

Your score ___

Alteration	Shot 1	Shot 2	Shot 3	Shot 4
Move ball back in stance	L H S F	L H S F	L H S F	L H S F
Move ball forward in stance	L H S F	L H S F	L H S F	L H S F
Grip down on club (hands closer to clubhead)	L H S F	L H S F	L H S F	L H S F
Swing harder (faster tempo)	L H S F	L H S F	L H S F	L H S F
Swing softer (slower tempo)	L H S F	L H S F	L H S F	L H S F

L = lower, H = higher, S = shorter, F = farther

Figure 9.2 Scorecard for alteration drill.

Wood Club Selection

Depending on the number of irons you decide to carry in your bag, you will have room for a larger or smaller number of woods. Most players have at least two woods—a driver and a 3-wood—in their bags and many players add a 5-wood and maybe a 7-wood if they decide to take out some of the longer irons.

A wood is typically used off the tee since that is when you want the ball to travel as far as possible. Of course, it is also important to keep the ball straight. When a straight shot becomes more important, players reevaluate and choose a club they feel confident will put the ball on the fairway. For some players, that means using a higher-numbered wood than the driver, which is the wood most commonly used off the tee. For others, it means selecting a lower-numbered iron instead.

As when choosing an iron, when you are not playing from the tee it is important to assess the conditions when choosing a wood. The lie, weather, landing area, and type of shot needed will guide your decision as to what wood to use (figure 9.3). The farther you want the ball to fly, the lower the number of wood you should use. If the ball is in a good lie on the fairway, an experienced player could use a driver; otherwise an iron is easier to hit. The more lofted the club is, the higher the number is.

Figure 9.3   Selecting a Wood Club

1. A longer shaft means a longer swing arc, which means faster clubhead speed

2. Commonly used woods are 1 (driver), 3, and 5; also popular are 4, 7, and 9

3. Address the ball opposite the forward heel with the feet a little farther apart

4. Keep the ball high, especially when using the driver

5. Swing just as in a regular swing

6. Since the ball is toward the forward heel, you will sweep the ball off the fairway or off the tee

Misstep

You top the ball when swinging at it with the wood.

Correction

When the club reaches the ball, it has already reached its lowest point. If you top the ball, the ball is probably too far forward in the stance. Move the ball back toward the middle of the stance. A general rule is to keep the ball opposite the inside of the left heel. If that does not help, try moving the ball back a little more, but never farther back than the middle of the stance.

Wood Drill 1. *The Wood-Picker*

Pick out the woods in your bag except for the driver. Say you have 3-, 5-, and 7-woods. Select three targets on the driving range that are reasonable distances for the three clubs. Your goal is to hit three good shots in a row with each club (you decide on the definition of a good shot). After you have hit three good shots, that club is out. If you hit two good shots and then miss the third, you have to start over. Count how many total shots it takes you to hit three good shots in a row. Divide this number by the number of woods you have to get the average number of shots it takes per club. The best possible average is three shots per club. Your goal is to hit three good shots per club in no more than 12 total shots.

To Decrease Difficulty

- Settle for two good shots in a row instead of three.
- Lower your standards for what makes a good shot.

To Increase Difficulty

- Try to hit four good shots in a row instead of three.
- Raise your standards for what makes a good shot.

Success Check

- Decide how to hit the shot before stepping up to the ball.
- Stick to your tempo.

Score Your Success

13 shots or more per club = 0 points

12 to 11 shots = 1 point

10 to 9 shots = 2 points

8 to 7 shots = 3 points

6 to 5 shots = 4 points

4 to 3 shots = 5 points

Your score ___

Wood Drill 2. *The Transporter*

A wood is often used to move the ball along the fairway, for example, on a par-5 hole when the green cannot be reached. When you use a wood in this way, accuracy is more important than distance. The distance goal may be to get the ball as far as possible, but in terms of accuracy you definitely want to keep the ball on the fairway.

In this drill, think about a hole you played where you used a wood to move the ball on the fairway. Think of how wide the fairway was and use that as a boundary to visualize a fairway on the driving range. Hit 10 balls on the driving range. Give yourself 3 points for hitting the right spot on the imaginary fairway, 2 points for hitting the fairway but not on the right spot, and 1 point for hitting the first cut of the rough.

To Decrease Difficulty

- Use a wider fairway.
- Use a higher-numbered wood.

To Increase Difficulty

- Use a narrower fairway.
- Find two different holes and alternate between them.

Success Check

- Be specific when you decide how to hit the shot. Make sure you know what you want to do and how to do it.
- Execute the shot as planned.

Score Your Success

0 to 6 points = 1 point

7 to 12 points = 2 points

13 to 18 points = 3 points

19 to 24 points = 4 points

25 to 30 points = 5 points

Your score ___

Tee Shot Club Selection

When you select a club for a tee shot, consider these factors:

- What is a good landing area for the tee shot?
- From where would you like to play your next shot?
- What is more important, distance or accuracy? How will this affect your choice of club?
- Are there hazards or other obstacles that you definitely want to avoid? Can you select a club that will avoid these hazards or obstacles?

The most common club to use off the tee is the driver (figure 9.4). The driver will get the ball to travel the farthest distance, so it is the most logical choice off the tee. The driver's loft, usually between 8 and 11 degrees, will create the most sidespin in the ball. Loft is the angle between the clubface and a line at a 90-degree angle from the surface.

Figure 9.4 **Selecting a Club for the Tee Shot**

1. Hit the tee shot with the driver unless hazards or other obstacles prevent it
2. Tee the ball up high
3. Place the ball toward the forward heel in the stance
4. Use a normal swing and sweep the ball off the tee

Misstep

You keep missing fairways and hitting shots way off target.

Correction

The best way to hit a long shot off the tee is not to muscle the ball to the fairway but to hit the ball with the sweet spot of the club. Reduce your tempo and focus on making a solid swing and good ball contact.

Tee Club Drill 1. *Last Golfer Standing*

This is a perfect drill for two or more people. Use a tee box on the driving range and choose two markers on the field to use as an imaginary fairway (one on each side of the fairway). Using the driver, hit one ball at a time and then switch players. As long as you hit the fairway, you stay in the game. The last golfer standing is the winner of the game. If you are alone, simply count the number of fairways you hit in a row. Your goal should be to hit at least eight fairways in a row.

To Decrease Difficulty

* Make the fairway wider.
* Use an iron instead of the driver.

To Increase Difficulty

* Make the fairway narrower.
* Ask a friend to try to disturb your focus, for example by talking to you during the backswing.

Success Check

* Make a distinct decision on which shot to hit at which target.
* Trust your body during the swing and keep your focus on the target.

Score Your Success

0 to 1 fairways = 0 points

2 to 3 fairways = 1 point

4 to 5 fairways = 2 points

6 to 7 fairways = 3 points

8 to 9 fairways = 4 points

10 or more fairways = 5 points

Your score ___

Tee Club Drill 2. *The Tee Shooter*

Think back to your favorite course or any course you are familiar with. On the driving range, picture a par-4 or par-5 hole on the course as vividly as possible. Visualize where the hazards and the obstacles on the hole would be and where the fairway and your ideal landing area would be. Pick your club and hit your shot. Your goal is to hit the visualized landing area on the driving range. Hit 10 balls. Give yourself 3 points each time you hit your intended landing area, 2 points if you miss your area but hit the fairway, 1 point if you miss the fairway but avoid obstacles such as trees or other hazards that would prevent you from hitting a normal second shot, and 0 points if you put the ball in a hazard.

To Decrease Difficulty

* Pick an easy hole where you can hit a club that you feel comfortable with.
* Pick a hole with as few obstacles as possible.

To Increase Difficulty

* Use five different holes so that you hit to the same target, or visualized landing area, only twice.
* Hit a couple of iron shots in between every tee shot.

Success Check

* Be specific when you decide how to play the shot. Make sure you know what you want to do and how to do it.
* Execute the shot as planned.

Score Your Success

0 to 6 points = 1 point

7 to 12 points = 2 points

13 to 18 points = 3 points

19 to 24 points = 4 points

25 to 30 points = 5 points

Your score ___

CLUB SELECTION STRATEGY

When it comes to club selection, strategic thinking is crucial. Good players have a hundred different ways to use each club in the bag. The type of shot and club depend on the situation at hand and the conditions of the course. Is there a need for a high shot, low shot, curved shot, bump and run, or shot that stops quickly after landing? Again, the answer to the question "what" lies in understanding what the present circumstances will do to the ball. Say that the pin is tucked in behind a bunker on the right side, the green is fairly firm, and a light breeze is blowing left to right. The ball is resting nicely on the fairway. A good player in this situation would most certainly try to hit a high shot with a club that would carry the ball over the bunker and at the same time give the ball enough spin for it to stop on the green. The player would aim left of the flag and let the wind or a smooth fade (curve from left to right) move the ball toward the pin. The player would much rather end up left of the pin than right of it with the risk of missing the green on the wrong side (with the pin on the right of the green, a shot from the green-side rough on the right would probably be much more difficult than from the left).

The next question, "how" to execute a shot like that, may require a bit of training to accomplish. You can accomplish any of these shots by changing clubs, but you can also execute them by changing the way you hit different clubs. Ask yourself the following questions:

- What do I want to do with the shot?
- What shot is called for?
- How is the shot executed?
- Am I skilled at this shot?
- What club and what swing or technique do I need to use to hit this shot?

Club Selection Strategy Drill 1. *Course Roulette*

Play nine holes on a golf course. While playing, give yourself different shots and lies than those you usually have. For instance, on a 350-yard (320-meter) par-4 hole, hit the tee shot with a 7-iron to leave yourself a different approach shot. Every time you leave yourself a different shot within two clubs off your normal club and you still hit the green, give yourself 2 points. Give yourself 1 point for hitting to a chip lie or a green-side bunker.

Success Check

- Carefully plan and execute your shots even if you are not using the club and distance you would normally use.
- Evaluate each shot and use that knowledge in your next shot.

Score Your Success

0 to 1 point = 0 points

2 to 4 points = 1 point

5 to 7 points = 2 points

8 to 11 points = 3 points

12 to 14 points = 4 points

15 points or more = 5 points

Your score ___

Club Selection Strategy Drill 2. *Target and Club Me*

Team up with a partner who is at roughly the same skill level as you. On the driving range, take turns selecting a target and club for each other. Hit to the target your partner has selected with the club your partner has selected. Give yourself 3 points if you hit the target with what you think is a good shot, 2 points if you hit the target but do not feel you hit a good shot, 1 point if you miss the target with what you think is a good shot, and 0 points if you miss the target and hit a bad shot. Hit 10 shots each.

To Decrease Difficulty

- Use only two different clubs for the 10 shots.
- Play with a partner who is not as skilled as you are.

To Increase Difficulty

- Put big gaps between the targets and clubs you use. For example, first use a wedge and then a 3-wood.
- Play with a partner who is better than you are.

Success Check

- Figure out a way to take the ball to the target even if the club is not one you would normally use.
- Stick to your decision and execute the shot according to the plan.

Score Your Success

0 to 6 points = 1 point

7 to 12 points = 2 points

13 to 18 points = 3 points

19 to 24 points = 4 points

25 to 30 points = 5 points

Your score ___

SELECTING CLUBS SUCCESS SUMMARY

Selecting clubs is a matter of understanding two things: Different clubs do different things with the ball and each club can be used many different ways. Selecting a club means not only reacting to the conditions or the yardage at hand but also deciding what type of shot to hit. The more ways you can use the clubs, the better prepared you will be for each lie.

Record your point totals from each of the drills in this step and add them up. If you scored at least 30 points, you have mastered this step and are ready to move on to the next. If you scored 20 to 29 points, you should be able to move on to the next step after reviewing and practicing a bit more, focusing on the drills where you scored low. If you scored fewer than 20 points, review the step again and practice the drills a few more times before moving on to the next step.

Iron Club Drills

   1. The Stepladder   ___ out of 5

   2. The Triple   ___ out of 5

   3. Alteration Drill   ___ out of 5

Wood Drills

   1. The Wood-Picker   ___ out of 5

   2. The Transporter   ___ out of 5

Tee Club Drills

   1. Last Golfer Standing   ___ out of 5

   2. The Tee Shooter   ___ out of 5

Club Selection Strategy Drills

   1. Course Roulette   ___ out of 5

   2. Target and Club Me   ___ out of 5

Total   ___ **out of 45**

Understanding club selection is a crucial part of golf. Why else would a player carry around as many as 14 clubs? As you develop as a golfer, you will find infinite ways to hit a golf ball and use a golf club. This is one of the reasons it takes quite a bit of practice to become an accomplished golfer. Now it is time to move on to using these different alternatives on the golf course. This is when course management, the next step, becomes crucial.

Managing the Course

If your hard work in developing your golf skills is going to pay off in low scores and successful rounds, you must learn to effectively manage your game on the golf course. In this step, you will learn how to fit your skills to a course by developing a plan to guide your decision making on each hole.

Good course management lets you use your skills to move the ball from tee to green in the fewest strokes no matter what par the hole is. Good course management also lets you successfully navigate any challenges presented by the course designer—doglegs, water hazards, bunkers, hilly fairways, or fast greens.

KNOW YOUR GAME

Good course management requires the ability to match your game to a particular golf course in order to shoot the lowest scores, so you must know both your game and the course well. The better you know both, the better you will be able to match your game to the course.

Knowing your game begins with knowing which skills are strengths and which are weaknesses. Begin by knowing the range of yardages you hit with each club. You can calculate this on a driving range by hitting 10 balls with each club in your bag. Record where each of the 10 balls lands and then take the average distance by adding the yardages and dividing the sum by 10 (table 10.1). You can use this knowledge on the course so that, for example, you know which club will carry a ball 140 yards over water to a green.

Next, look at every club in your bag and gauge your success with each one. Success is determined by your ability to land the ball on an intended target 75 percent of the time. Some players use a scale of 1 to 10, with 10 meaning they can hit the target 10 out of 10 times with that club. Record this information in table 10.1. The clubs with the highest rates of success should be used whenever possible in your round, and those with the lowest rates of success should receive the most attention during practice. For example, if your success with a driver is rated 3 but your 3-metal is rated 5, the 3-metal should be the club of choice for most tee shots. One of the professional golfers we work with, Richard S. Johnson, recently replaced a driving iron with a 5-metal. He hit both clubs the same distance but found he had greater accuracy with the 5-metal. One of the reasons that Richard is a successful touring professional is that he knows which clubs give him the most success in a given situation.

Now look at the shots you have practiced and rate your success with these shots. Look at your scoring summaries in previous steps to find strengths and weaknesses, or use the same scale of 1 to 10 that you used for assessing clubs. By understanding your skills in putting, chipping, pitching, iron and wood play, and bunker play, you will know which shots to hit in a given situation. For example, if you are a better bunker player than a pitcher from the rough and you find yourself in tall rough behind a green with a bunker in front, you would know to err on the side of being short with the approach rather than long.

While honest assessments can often be hard on the ego (golf is, after all, a difficult game), they are imperative to finding success on the golf course. An accurate appraisal of your skills will allow you to set realistic expectations, play successfully within your limitations, and know when to be conservative and when to get aggressive.

Table 10.1 Club Yardage and Success Ratings

Club	1	2	3	4	5	6	7	8	9	10	Average	Success rating
Lob wedge												
Sand wedge												
Pitching wedge												
9-iron												
8-iron												
7-iron												
6-iron												
5-iron												
4-iron												
3-iron												
Fairway wood												
Driver												
Other												

Know Your Game Drill 1. *Yardage Guide*

In this exercise, you will gauge your skill with each iron and metal club. This is an important exercise if you are to effectively manage your game.

Choose a day with no wind or rain to perform this drill. On a flat driving range, identify an imaginary line running from you out through the driving range. It helps if there are at least three yardage markers on the range to help you gauge the distance of each shot. Begin with your highest-lofted wedge and finish with your lowest-lofted metal club. Hit 10 balls with each club.

For each club, note the average distance the ball traveled in the air, the average distance the ball finished left or right of the line (dispersion), and your tendency to hit fade (left of the line) or draw (right of the line) shots. Record the data in table 10.2. Don't worry about how far your ball rolls forward. Many factors influence ball roll, such as ground moisture, grass type and length, elevation, and ball spin, and most of these factors are beyond your control. It is much more important to know how far in the air each of your clubs carries the ball.

Score Your Success

Give yourself 2 points for every club for which you calculate an average air yardage.

Your score ___

Table 10.2   Yardage Guide

Club	Average air distance	Average dispersion	Fade or draw
Lob wedge			
Sand wedge			
Pitching wedge			
9-iron			
8-iron			
7-iron			
6-iron			
5-iron			
4-iron			
3-iron			
Fairway wood			
Driver			
Other			

Know Your Game Drill 2. *My Most Successful Shots*

All golfers need to know which parts of their game are the strongest and which are the weakest so that they can play to their strengths and practice their weaknesses until they become strengths. In this exercise, rate your golfing skills from 1 to 8 with 1 being your best skill and 8 being your weakest. Record the information in figure 10.1.

Skill	Rating (1 = highest, 8 = lowest)
Bunker play	
Chipping	
Full swing with fairway woods	
Full swing with irons	
Pitching	
Putting	
Shots from the rough	
Tee shots with driver	

Figure 10.1   Skill assessment.

Score Your Success

Give yourself 1 point for every shot you rated.

   Your score ___

KNOW THE COURSE

Once you have an accurate understanding of your capabilities with the clubs, you are ready to take your game to the course. Golf is played one hole at a time, one stroke at a time. Keep that in mind when planning your course strategy.

   The best way to plan a course strategy is by starting backward. In other words, begin with the hole and work back to the green. Ask yourself where on the green would be the best place for a putt (usually you want a straight, uphill putt). This will tell you where to land your approach shot. Once you know that spot, ask yourself where on the fairway would be the best place to hit the approach shot. The answer to this question will help you get past hazards or high rough and land your tee shot where you want it to go. For example, on a par-4 hole in which the hole is cut behind a bunker on the left side of the green, you will want to place the tee shot on the right side of the fairway to give you a better angle to the green so that you don't have to hit a shot over the bunker (figure 10.2).

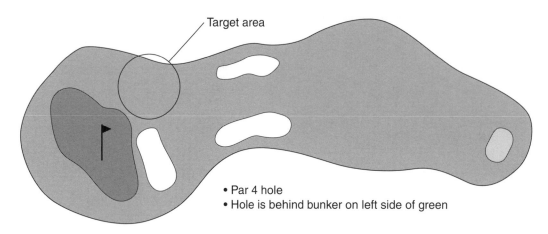

Target area

• Par 4 hole
• Hole is behind bunker on left side of green

Figure 10.2   For this par-4 hole, put the tee shot on the right side of the fairway.

In addition to your skills, course strategy will be influenced by distance, hole features such as hazards and hills, and weather.

Distance

The best way to play a hole is very much influenced by the distance to the hole. In some cases, it is wise to ignore the par rating for the hole and simply calculate your chance of success based on the overall distance. For example, a par-3 hole may be 210 yards (192 meters) long and surrounded by deep bunkers (figure 10.3). Do you have a club that will reliably and accurately carry the ball that distance or would it be better

to hit a tee shot 150 yards to a landing area and then pitch the ball 60 yards to the hole? If the par-3 hole has deep bunkers, rough, or a water hazard around the hole, the second option may result in the lower score. You will avoid making bogey, and you may even have a chance for par on a difficult par-3 hole. This was the strategy Billy Casper used on the longest par-3 hole of the 1959 U.S. Open Championship. Rather than trying to blast the ball to the hole 216 yards (198 meters) away, he laid up, hit a well-practiced chip shot, and putted in for par on the third hole at Winged Foot all four days of the tournament, and he won the championship.

- Par 3 hole, 210 yards
- Hole surrounded by bunkers

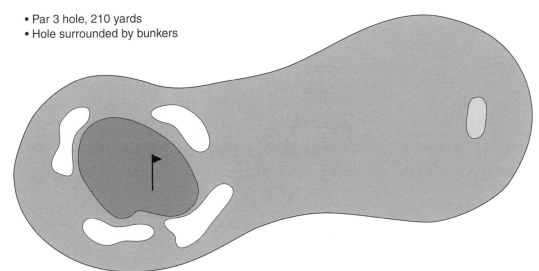

Figure 10.3 On a par-3 hole that is 210 yards long, are you better off trying to hit the ball 210 yards from the tee or hitting it 150 yards from the tee and then pitching it 60 yards to the hole?

The same strategy applies on par-4 or par-5 holes. Hit only those shots you feel are within your comfort range for distance. It does little good to hit a drive 300 yards (274 meters) if the ball gets into trouble. It is always better to attempt a slightly longer shot from the fairway than a shorter shot from behind a tree, from the rough, or out of the water.

When standing on the tee box, consider the total distance to the hole and then decide which series of clubs will give you the greatest chance of success. For example, on a 400-yard (366-meter) par-4 hole, it may make more sense to hit a 150-yard tee shot, a second 150-yard shot, and then a 100-yard shot to the green (figure 10.4). If one of those three shots (or even all of them)

veers a little left or right, the ball most likely will not find serious danger and you will still be on the green in three shots with a chance to make a putt for par.

Playing for a comfortable distance has the added advantage of letting you play in a comfort zone. That is, you will swing more freely and with more control when you are attempting to hit a shot that you feel you can easily make. Attempting to hit the ball a long way to a small target makes most amateur golfers swing too hard, which has an adverse effect on timing and control. In other words, it is more difficult to make a good shot when attempting to hit a ball too far. Play comfortable.

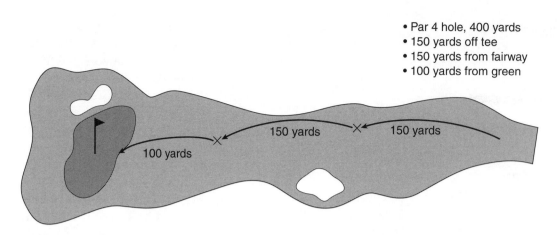

- Par 4 hole, 400 yards
- 150 yards off tee
- 150 yards from fairway
- 100 yards from green

150 yards   150 yards

100 yards

Figure 10.4 For a 400-yard par-4 hole, this golfer chose to hit a 150-yard shot off the tee, a 150-yard shot from the fairway, and a 100-yard shot to the green.

Once your ball is in the fairway, you must determine the distance for your next shot. All golf courses have yardage markers, which are measured from the middle of the green to specific places in the fairway. Standard markers on most courses are placed 100, 150, and 200 yards (91, 137, and 183 meters) from the middle of the green. On many golf courses, the yardages to the middle of the green are also marked on the sprinkler heads. To determine how far your ball lies from the middle of the green, a common practice is to step off your yardage; that is, find the closest yardage marker to your ball and count the number of steps from there to your ball. If you can take a step of approximately one yard, simply add or subtract the number of paces to the yardage marker distance to determine the distance your lie is from the middle of the green. This is invaluable information for knowing which club to choose for your next shot. The step off

drill (page 129) is a good drill for practicing this skill and establishing the length of stride you will need to step off yardage.

Professional golfers consider from what location they want to hit the approach shot to the green and then choose the club for the tee shot that will get them to that spot in the fairway. That strategy helps them make a living at this game, and it will work for you, too.

A final thought on distance as a factor in course management—take enough club. Most golfers overestimate the distance they hit a club and the consistency with which they strike the ball. Unless you consistently drive the ball through the fairway or hit over the green, err on the side of a stronger club. In other words, choose a club you are confident will make the ball travel the distance it needs to go and perhaps even a bit farther.

Misstep

You don't take enough club, causing the shot to fall short of the target.

Correction

Underclubbing is one of the most common errors golfers make. Know the distances you hit each club and always be sure you have enough club to reach the target landing area.

Misstep

You take too much club off the tee and do not find the fairway or green.

Correction

The most important goal from the teeing ground is to put the ball in play by hitting the green or fairway. Use the club that will get the ball to the green or the fairway rather than the club that will hit the ball the farthest.

Hole Features

To give definition, challenge, and beauty to a hole, golf course designers structure the hole with a variety of features, including hills; water such as ponds, lakes, or the ocean; sand or grass bunkers; trees; sand waste areas; and grass. The designer can also vary the routing patterns that turn the hole left or right from the teeing ground. These features are called doglegs because from an aerial view, the fairway appears to be shaped like a dog's leg.

While most designers prefer to use the natural characteristics of the land when designing a course, they often add a few features to each hole. In managing the course and planning your strategy for a hole, you need to consider these features. We will discuss these features in terms of the greatest effect they can have on your score, as this determines the feature's importance in your decision making.

Pay particular attention to any white stakes you see on the hole; they mark the out-of-bounds area. If you hit the ball to or past these stakes, you incur a one-stroke penalty in addition to the stroke you took to hit the ball out of bounds. You must replay the shot from the original position, so you lose both a stroke and distance. When choosing a landing area on the hole, make sure you are well clear of the out-of-bounds area.

Next, consider areas on the hole where you might lose your ball or find yourself with an unplayable lie. These areas are usually covered with heavy brush, bushes, or tall grass. The penalty for losing a ball is the same as the penalty for going out of bounds. An unplayable lie results in a one-stroke penalty and a drop two club lengths from where the ball lies or a return to the original spot where the ball was played. Hitting a ball to these areas will increase your score, so play away from them.

Water hazards (figure 10.5) cause most players a great deal of anxiety, so the natural tendency is to avoid these areas. Water hazards are marked with yellow stakes and lateral water hazards are marked with red stakes. If you hit your ball into a water hazard, you can drop your ball behind the water hazard or next to a lateral hazard, so you don't lose distance that you would with a lost or out-of-bounds ball. If forced to chose between hitting close to white stakes or red stakes, red stakes will hurt you less.

Although it's best to avoid severe rough, woods, or waste areas such as sandy or rocky areas not maintained by course personnel, if your ball does land in one of these areas you can play your next shot without penalty as long as you do not have an unplayable lie. It will not be easy to make this shot, however, since the conditions make it difficult to have an unobstructed shot to the green or fairway. When playing from

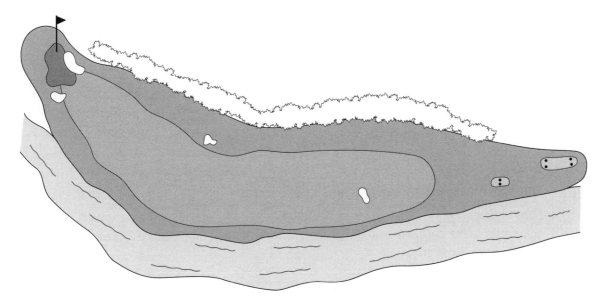

Figure 10.5 Don't fear water hazards. Hitting into a water hazard is less harmful to your score than hitting the ball out of bounds or losing a ball in the rough.

one of these areas, your first priority should be to get the ball back in play, which usually means playing it back to the fairway with a pitch or chip shot. Realize that you have made an error, but don't compound the error by demanding too much of your next shot. Just get yourself out of trouble.

Misstep

You fail to get out of trouble.

Correction

When you get into trouble—when the ball is behind a tree, in a bunker, or in deep rough, for example—make your first priority getting the ball back to the fairway. Don't make a bad situation worse by trying for too much.

Bunkers are the next feature to consider. A bunker will permit a good stance and a clean strike at the ball, so better players generally prefer playing out of a bunker over playing from deep rough (figure 10.6). While you will not be penalized for having to play out of a bunker, it is better to be on the fairway or the green if possible. Because of their size and color contrast as well as the fear most players have of being in the bunker, course designers place bunkers in strategic locations to add challenge and character to a hole. Perhaps it is stating the obvious to advise you to play away from bunkers, but on a very difficult hole a bunker may be a better option than risking running into other course features such as out of bounds or heavy rough.

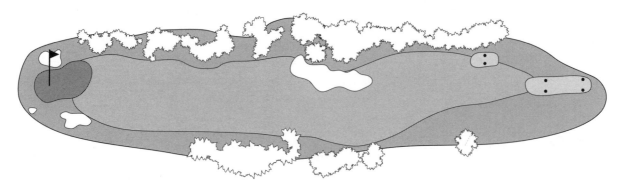

Figure 10.6 You can hit out of a bunker without penalty, so it is an acceptable option if you are concerned about hitting the ball out of bounds or into heavy rough.

Misstep

You consistently land in bunkers and other hazards.

Correction

Study the holes carefully in order to play away from trouble, even if it means being a little farther from the hole.

Course designers use slopes, hills, and mounds for strategic and aesthetic purposes on a golf hole. Many players have difficulty hitting the ball from anything other than a flat lie, so consider the best place to land on the fairway or green. Look for flat lies in the fairways. When hitting to the green, leave yourself either a straight putt or one that is slightly uphill.

Misstep

You miss the green close to the hole and have little room to land or roll the ball before it reaches the hole. This is known as missing the green on the wrong side or short-siding yourself.

Correction

If a hole is cut close to the edge of a green, play to the middle of the green rather than to the flag.

Finally, course designers use the width and angle of the holes to provide definition and character. You should take into account the width of the fairway or green when choosing a club. A narrow fairway usually means a shorter hole, so perhaps a fairway wood or even an iron off the tee is called for. A fairway that is generously wide is probably longer and will require a club that can carry the ball farther even if you hit the club with less accuracy. Narrow greens require more accurate shots, usually with a higher trajectory so the ball will stop sooner on the green. When planning your approach shot to the green, choose a club that will accomplish these two purposes, accuracy and loft.

If the fairway turns to the left or right, making the hole invisible from the tee box, the hole is a dogleg (figure 10.7). (From an aerial view, the fairway appears to be shaped like a dog's leg.) When facing a dogleg, consider risk and reward. The closer you can put the ball to the turn in the fairway, the closer you will be to the hole; however, often you will also be closer to danger because course designers usually place bunkers, trees, or waste areas near the turn. Determine your comfort zone when playing a shot near to or away from the turn. If the risk appears greater than the reward, play conservatively. If the risk appears minimal—you can drive the ball over the bunker or shape your shot around the trees—the reward may make the risk worth taking. In general, a conservative strategy is better for avoiding high scores.

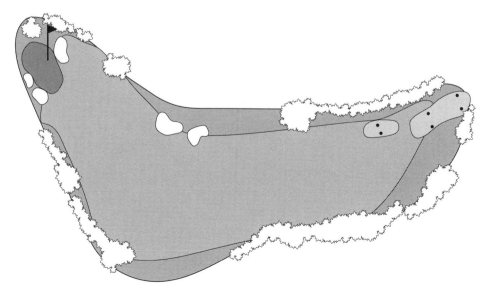

Figure 10.7 Consider the risks and rewards of hitting close to the turn on a doglegged fairway.

Strategic Importance of Hole Features

1. Out of bounds
2. Lost ball and unplayable lie
3. Water hazards
4. Severe rough, waste areas, woods
5. Bunkers
6. Hills, slopes, mounds
7. Shape of the fairway and green

Weather

Golf is an outdoor sport. The only weather condition that halts play is lightning, so you will need to factor weather conditions into your course strategy.

In general, wind affects the flight of the ball more than any other weather condition. A gusty day can make for a long game on the golf course. Wind affects a ball's ability to carry and the direction the ball is going. If you hit into the wind, the ball will not carry as far; if you hit downwind, particularly with a club that lofts the ball high into the air, the ball will carry much farther. When selecting a club for a shot, consider the strength of the wind and its direction. For example, a 150-yard (137-meter) shot may actually play more like a 170-yard (155-meter) shot if you are hitting it into a strong wind (figure 10.8).

The direction of the ball is also affected by the wind and you will need to adjust your club and shot accordingly. A left-to-right wind can send a well-struck tee shot from the middle of the fairway into the middle of a lake (figure 10.9). Determining precisely how much effect

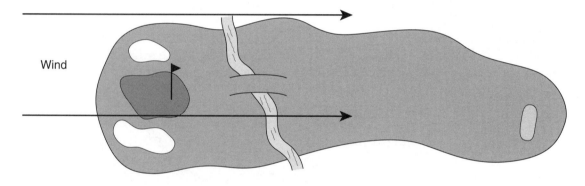

Figure 10.8 Hitting into a strong wind can make a 150-yard shot feel like a 170-yard shot.

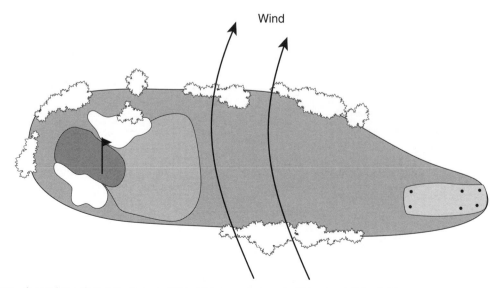

Figure 10.9 A good tee shot may go awry if it is hit into a strong wind blowing left to right.

the wind has on the ball is part experience and part guesswork, but in general wind will affect the ball more than you think, so play for it. Look at the tops of the trees or the flag on the green or toss some grass into the air to gauge the speed and direction of the wind.

A golf ball doesn't travel as far in cold weather or in rainy conditions. These elements will also affect your grip. A hand warmer on a cold day and a dry towel on a rainy day are good accessories to have on the course. Conversely, on hot, dry days the ball will travel farther. If the fairway or green have baked in the hot sun for several days, the ball will roll much more than normal.

Although it is not a weather condition, elevation also will affect a golf ball. The higher the elevation, the farther the golf ball will travel. Make adjustments for these conditions before striking the ball.

Know the Course Drill 1. *Hole Strategy*

The golf hole in figure 10.10 is a relatively short par 4, but it has several hazards. Plan your strategy for this hole. Place a *T* where you would like your tee shot to stop and in parentheses identify the club you would use to hit that shot. Next, place an *A* where you would like your approach shot to land on the green and in parentheses identify the club you would use to hit that shot.

Score Your Success

Using your distance chart in table 10.1 (page 120), give yourself 2 points for each shot that avoided going over the hazards and 2 points for each shot that used the club that would get your ball to that spot.

Your score ___

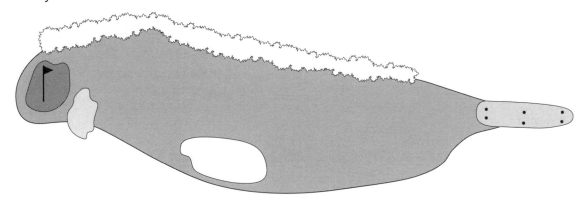

Figure 10.10 For this par-4 hole, place a *T* where you would like your tee shot to land and an *A* where you would like your approach shot to land on the green.

Know the Course Drill 2. *Step Off*

Take a tape measure and extend it for 5 yards on a flat surface. Straddle the tape measure and take steps so that your strides are as close to 1 yard in length as possible (measured from the middle of your feet). In five steps, you should be at 5 yards. This often takes practice, so repeat it 10 times.

Next, pick a hole on a practice green and step off distances from that hole to 5, 10, and 20 yards. Use golf balls to mark the distances as you step them off and then use the tape measure to check your accuracy. Repeat the drill three times from three different holes for a total of 9 yardage stepoffs.

Score Your Success

Give yourself 1 point for each measure that is within 24 inches (.61 meters) of the stepped-off distance and 2 points for each measure within 18 inches (.46 meters). For example, if you have stepped off a distance of 10 yards (30 feet) and it measures 31 feet, you score 2 points.

Your score ___

129

Know the Course Drill 3. *Phantom Threesome*

From a practice tee, imagine a par-4 hole with a fairway hazard such as water on the left or a bunker on the right and a green-side hazard such as a bunker or deep rough. Use objects such as flags or mounds on the driving range to shape your hole. Play the hole as an imaginary three-some, portraying three different players using three different strategies. Imagine you are a long hitter, then a shot maker, and then a short-hitting, conservative player. Tee off as the long hitter first, then the shot maker, and then the conservative player. Play each ball onto the imaginary green from the practice tee as if you were actually play-ing the course as a threesome. After completing the first hole, imagine a par-5 hole with hazards and play that hole. Repeat until you complete nine holes. For each shot, give yourself 3 points for determining the distance the shot will travel, 1 point for considering the hazards on the imaginary hole, and 1 point for taking into account the wind and other weather conditions, for a maximum of 5 points per shot and 15 points per hole.

To Decrease Difficulty

- Play the round as a single player.
- Design imaginary golf holes with wide fairways and no hazards.

To Increase Difficulty

- Include two fairway hazards on each hole.
- Imagine the holes as you would find them on your favorite golf course.

Success Check

- For each shot, consider shot distance, hole features, and weather conditions.

Score Your Success

Fewer than 35 points = 0 points

35 to 54 points = 2 points

55 to 74 points = 4 points

75 to 94 points = 6 points

95 to 114 points = 8 points

115 to 135 points = 10 points

Your score ___

Know the Course Drill 4. *Identify the Trouble*

List the trouble areas of the hole shown in figure 10.11. Rank the trouble spots from 1 to 5, with 1 being the area most likely to result in a higher score. Give yourself 5 points for each correct ranking. (Answers appear on page 134.)

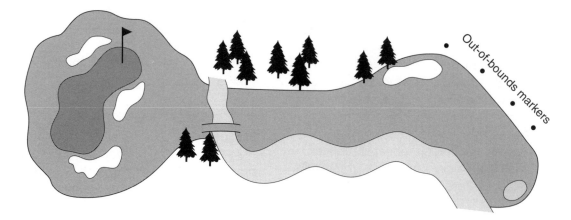

Figure 10.11   Rank the trouble spots for this hole in order from most to least dangerous.

1. _____
2. _____
3. _____
4. _____
5. _____

Know the Course Drill 5. *Manage the Entire Hole*

Good course management requires you to match your playing strengths to the hole's weaknesses. For each of the holes shown in figures 10.13, 10.14, and 10.15, mark an X on an appropriate target landing area for each shot. Identify the club you would use to hit the ball to the target by placing a symbol beside the X such as 8i for an 8-iron, 5m for a 5-metal, SW for a sand wedge, or D for a driver. Figure 10.12 shows a sample hole already filled in. (Answers for figures 10.13, 10.14, and 10.15 appear on page 134.)

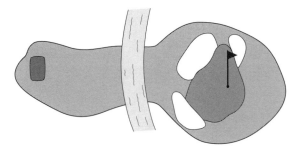

Figure 10.14   Hole 2, 168 yards, par 3.

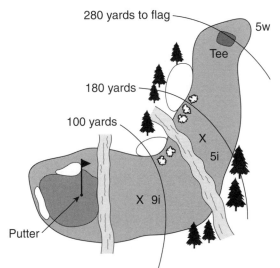

Figure 10.12   Sample hole.

Figure 10.15   Hole 3, 502 yards, par 5.

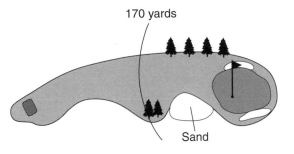

Figure 10.13   Hole 1, 341 yards, par 4.

Know the Course Drill 6.   *Managing Your Round*

The better your strategy, the greater your chance of success. In figure 10.16, plot your strategy for each hole as you did in the previous drill, indicating the landing area and the club you would use for each shot. After completing this exercise using figure 10.16, get a scorecard from your favorite course and repeat the drill, then go play a round and compare your plan with your actual play. (Answers appear on page 135.)

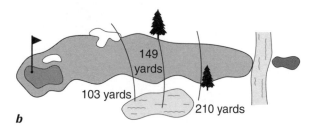

a

Hole 1, 254 yards (232 meters), par 4.

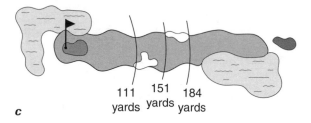

b

Hole 2, 410 yards (374 meters), par 5.

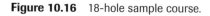

c

Hole 3, 340 yards (310 meters), par 4.

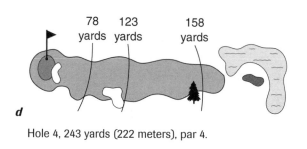

d

Hole 4, 243 yards (222 meters), par 4.

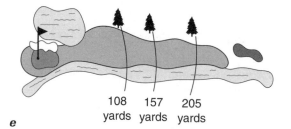

e

Hole 5, 300 yards (274 meters), par 4.

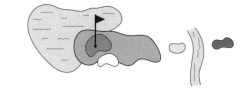

f

Hole 6, 135 yards (123 meters), par 3.

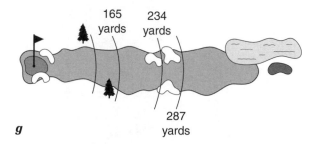

g

Hole 7, 490 yards (448 meters), par 5.

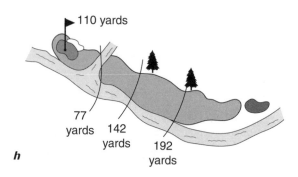

h

Hole 8, 366 yards (335 meters), par 4.

Figure 10.16   18-hole sample course.

i

Hole 9, 123 yards (113 meters), par 3.

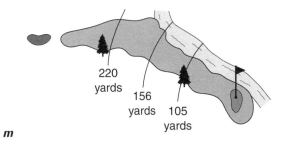

m

Hole 13, 410 yards (375 meters), par 4.

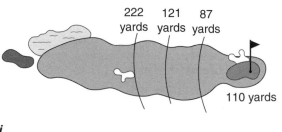

j

Hole 10, 475 yards (434 meters), par 5.

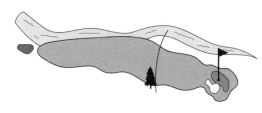

n

Hole 14, 310 yards (283 meters), par 4.

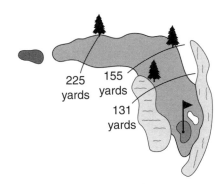

h

Hole 11, 400 yards (366 meters), par 4.

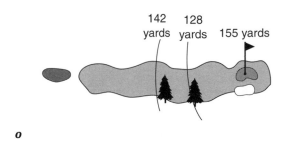

o

Hole 15, 235 yards (215 meters), par 4.

l

Hole 12, 120 yards (110 meters), par 3.

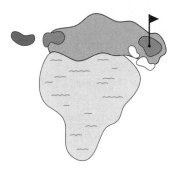

p

Hole 16, 122 yards (112 meters), par 3.

(continued)

(continued)

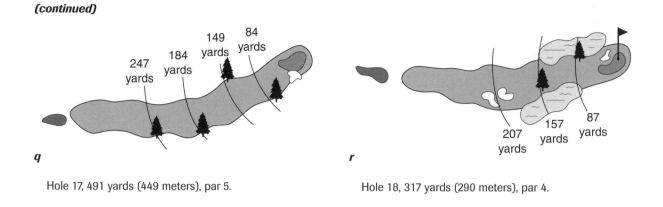

q

Hole 17, 491 yards (449 meters), par 5.

r

Hole 18, 317 yards (290 meters), par 4.

Score Your Success

Review your overall plan for all 18 holes and score yourself based on the following criteria:

If you attempted to play away from hazards = 5 points

If you first determined from where on the fairway you wanted to hit your approach shot as you determined your tee shots = 5 points

If you played to the middle of the green on each approach shot = 3 points

If on par-4 and par-5 holes you used more clubs than just your driver = 3 points

Your score ___

Answer Key

Answers for Know the Course Drill 4, *Identify the Trouble (page 130)*

1. Out of bounds
2. Lost ball or unplayable lie
3. Water

4. Woods
5. Bunker

Answers for Know the Course Drill 5, *Manage the Entire Hole (page 131)*

A well-designed golf hole will leave you many options. The clubs selected and types of shots hit will depend largely on your skill and ability to manage risks. A smart player accurately assesses his skill and plays the hole so as to minimize risks. The answers that follow are only suggestions based on our experiences with beginning and intermediate golfers. Compare your answers to

ours and evaluate the way you considered each factor for the hole.

Hole 1 (figure 10.13), par 4, 341 yards. Aim the tee shot to the middle of the fairway about 200 yards, short of the sand on the right and trees on the left. This will leave you a 140- to 150-yard approach shot to a large green.

Hole 2 (figure 10.14), par 3, 168 yards. With water before the green, large bunkers in front of the green, and the flag in the back part of the green, you need to select a club that will carry the ball at least 170 yards in the air to the middle of the green.

Hole 3 (figure 10.15), par 5, 502 yards. This hole will require three shots to reach the green. It is

better to play three low-risk shots. A 200-yard tee shot will get you over the lake and leave you short of the bunker, taking both hazards out of play. A second shot of 150 yards will get you to the middle of the fairway and leave you a third shot of 150 yards to the middle of the green.

Answers for Know the Course Drill 6, *Managing Your Round (page 132)*

The better your strategy in a round of golf, the greater your chance of success. In figure 10.16, plot your strategy for each hole in a similar pattern to the manage the entire hole drill. Indicate the landing area for each shot and identify the club you would use for the shot.

Hole 1, par 4, 254 yards. A 170-yard tee shot aimed for the left center of the fairway will take the bunker on the right out of play and leave you with an approach shot of fewer than 90 yards.

Hole 2, par 5, 410 yards. Aim the tee shot for the right side of the fairway to avoid the water on the left. A 200-yard tee shot will leave 210 yards to the hole. Aim the second shot for the middle of the fairway for a distance of 140 yards. This will take you past the bunker on the right and leave a pitch shot of 80 yards to the middle of the green.

Hole 3, par 4, 340 yards. Aim the tee shot just left of the bunker on the right side of the fairway. This will take the water on the left out of play. A tee shot of 200 yards will leave you with an approach shot of 140 yards. With water on the right side of the green, aim your approach shot for the left or center of the green.

Hole 4, par 4, 243 yards. With a small green guarded in front by a large bunker, an accurate approach shot is needed. Therefore it will be necessary to get the ball closer to the green with the tee shot. The only hazard facing you off the tee is a fairway bunker on the left. Using your 150-yard club, aim the tee shot to the right side of the fairway. This will leave you with a 93-yard approach shot.

Hole 5, par 4, 300 yards. The fairway is widest approximately 200 yards from the tee box; this

should be your landing area. Water runs the entire length of the left side of the fairway, so aim your tee shot to the right or center of the fairway. A good tee shot will leave you with a 100-yard approach shot. Bunkers and a water hazard line the right side of the green, and there is a water hazard to the left. Aim for the middle of the green.

Hole 6, par 3, 135 yards. The dangers on this hole come from the water that surrounds the right and back sides of the green and from the bunker on the front right. While an accurate shot to the middle of the green is optimal, the bailout area is short and slightly right. If your shot goes astray, a chip and pitch can save par. Select a club that will carry the ball no farther than 135 yards.

Hole 7, par 5, 490 yards. For a long hitter, this hole may be reachable in two shots. For the average player, it will take three shots to reach the green. The only serious trouble comes from the bunkers on the left and right sides of the fairway about 200 yards from the tee. A tee shot at 190 yards will take the bunkers out of play and leave you with 200 yards to the hole. A second shot of 125 yards would leave you with a full pitch shot of 75 yards to the middle of the green. A short three shot will help you avoid the bunkers guarding the green.

Hole 8, par 4, 366 yards. A tee shot of 200 yards aimed down the right or center will help you avoid the water on the left. Hit a 166-yard approach shot over water to the green guarded on the left by water. You will need to carry the ball at least 90 yards in the air to get over the water. There is a landing area over the water, so even if you are a bit short, you can still chip and putt for par. If you do not feel confident in getting the ball over the water, hit a 60-yard shot so it stops well before the water and make your third shot a 106-yard shot to the green. With the amount of water on this hole, it is better to reduce risk and play safely. Better a bogey than a high number.

Hole 9, par 3, 123 yards. With water on the left side of the green, aim to the right or center of the green with a club that will reach the hole.

Hole 10, par 5, 475 yards. A 200-yard drive will leave the average golfer short of the fairway bunker. A second shot of 150 to 175 yards to a wide fairway will leave a pitch or short iron approach to the green. A longer hitter could drive the ball down the left or center of the fairway to avoid the bunker, then use a fairway wood to get the second shot to the green.

Hole 11, par 4, 400 yards. This dogleg right hole is long and full of danger. Play safely to avoid errant shots or penalty strokes. A tee shot aimed toward the second pine tree on the left side of the fairway will leave you an open approach shot to the green. A drive of 200 yards still leaves 200 yards to the green. Consider laying up with a second shot of 125 yards, leaving you a 75-yard pitch shot to the green. This should effectively take the fairway water hazards out of play and help you gain a short approach shot to a green surrounded by water hazards and a bunker.

Hole 12, par 3, 120 yards. The front bunker guarding the green means you will need plenty of club to reach the green. Choose a club that will carry the bunker and get the ball all the way to the hole (your 125-yard club would be a good choice). With water on the right, aim left of center on the green.

Hole 13, par 4, 410 yards. A 225-yard tee shot hit to the right center of the fairway will give you a chance to reach the green with a long iron or fairway wood and keep you away from the water on the left. If this long par 4 leaves you with more than 200 yards to the green after the tee shot, consider a second shot of 150 yards, leaving you a pitch or short iron for an approach shot.

Hole 14, par 4, 310 yards. A 200-yard tee shot down the right side of the fairway will leave you with a middle or short iron approach. Be sure to take enough club to carry the bunker on your approach shot.

Hole 15, par 4, 235 yards. With a narrow fairway on this short hole, use a fairway metal (3-wood or 5-wood) off the tee for better accuracy. This will still leave you with a short iron to the hole.

Hole 16, par 3, 122 yards. Water and bunkers are on the right, so aim the tee shot left center of the green. Take enough club to get the ball to the hole.

Hole 17, par 5, 491 yards. A slight dogleg left means you can gain an advantage by aiming left or center with your tee shot. A 200-yard drive will leave you with a middle iron second shot (150 to 170 yards) and a middle or short iron approach shot (141 to 121 yards) to the middle of the green. Avoid the greenside bunker on the right by aiming slightly left of center.

Hole 18, par 4, 317 yards. This is a short hole but one wrought with danger. An accurate tee shot of 160 yards aimed just left of the fairway tree will get you past the fairway bunkers, keep you out of the water, and take the trees out of play. This will leave you with a 157-yard approach shot. Aim for the right side of the green to avoid the bunker guarding the left.

COURSE MANAGEMENT SUCCESS SUMMARY

When preparing for a tournament, professional golfers spend several days playing practice rounds on the tournament course. While playing these practice rounds, the players note the length and features of each hole and develop a strategy for the course. They know which clubs they will hit and to what landing areas. They also consider how their strategy may change due to weather or their tournament standing. For example, they may have an idea of alternative clubs to use in case the wind blows on a hole with water hazards or if a downhill fairway begins to dry out from a hot sun. Course management is one area of golf that you can easily play like a pro. Know your strengths, know the course, and plan a strategy that will help you find success on your scorecard.

Record your point totals from each of the drills in this step and add them together. If you scored at least 95 out of 117 points, you're ready for the next step. If you scored 70 to 94 points, you're almost there; move on after reviewing the sections you feel you can improve the most. If you scored fewer than 70 points, review the information and go through the drills again to raise your scores.

Know Your Game Drills

   1. Yardage Guide   ___ out of 26

   2. My Most Successful Shots   ___ out of 8

Know the Course Drills

   1. Hole Strategy   ___ out of 8

   2. Step Off   ___ out of 18

   3. Phantom Threesome   ___ out of 10

   4. Identify the Trouble   ___ out of 25

   5. Manage the Entire Hole   ___ out of 6

   6. Managing Your Round   ___ out of 16

Total   ___ *out of 117*

With the completion of this step, you have learned and practiced the essential skills of golf, from putting a ball into a hole to managing your game. You've come a long way and can now play golf competently. But like everyone who enjoys this wonderful game, you probably yearn to get even better. The next step will help you develop mental and emotional control on the course so that you can maintain your confidence throughout the round.

Maintaining Focus on the Course

"Golf is not a game of perfect," sport psychologist Bob Rotella states in his book of the same name (1995). For a long time, perhaps as long as you play golf, the not-so-perfect shots are going to outnumber the perfect ones. For this reason, knowing how to deal with not-so-great shots is just as important as knowing how to deal with good shots. What it comes down to is mental and emotional control and being able to stay in the psychological state in which you have the best possible chance to perform. That goes for the first shot as well as the last shot and every shot in between during a round or a tournament. To be the best golfer you can possibly be, you need to develop your shot-making skills as much as possible. But if you cannot access those skills when they are needed, such as on the last green or fairway during a tournament or on the first tee when the pressure is on, you will not be able to play your best. The best players in the world are great ball strikers and shot makers, but they are also great at performing those skills when it really matters. The world is full of golfers with great range swings and good practice or social round scores.

Finding flow, or the zone, that state where everything is effortless, is something we all do occasionally, usually without knowing how we actually got there. Learning how to find the zone often requires learning about yourself and how you think and what you see, hear, and feel when in the zone. It is also about learning how to practice this state and the formula that gets you there. It is not easy, but it can be done!

LEARN FROM THE PROS

To say that the top players in the world are good at following their winning formula is stating the obvious. Many golfers would agree that this is what distinguishes a world-class performer from an average tour player. Every player on the PGA and LPGA tour has outstanding shot-making skills, but only those who can access their full potential when the heat is on will prevail. That is when players like Annika Sörenstam, Tiger Woods, Vijay Singh, and a few others stand out from the rest.

To describe what these players do psychologically to perform so well is not easy. Individual differences are a factor; solutions that work for one golfer may not work for another. An American researcher, Deborah Graham, spent her doctoral thesis trying to find the psychological difference between the players who win on professional golf tours and the players who do not. She concentrated on LPGA tour players, but she also included a few players from the PGA tour. To standardize the procedure, she used a well-known personality test, the IPAT 16 or 16 PF, developed by a researcher named Catell. Graham found that champions commonly possess the following qualities:

- They have a narrow focus, which helps them gather their attention for every shot. They are also good at relaxing and broadening their attention in between shots.

- Their abstract-thinking skills are average or above, which helps them pick the right club, strategy, and tactics.

- They are emotionally stable, which means they show no or little reaction to good or bad shots.

- They show a higher level of dominance, which probably makes them more aggressive than others.

- Their attitude is tough, and they tend to care less about others than the average person does. They care about themselves and their game and they are tough on themselves when needed.

- They show a high level of self-confidence, and they do not stop believing in themselves even after playing badly.

- They have a high level of independence, which is an advantage when planning the game and picking the club to hit. Off the course this is a good characteristic as well since it helps them take responsibility for their lives and not let others bother them.

- Their level of arousal is somewhere between low and high. Parts of the game, such as putting, require low arousal while other parts require higher arousal. Generally speaking, too little arousal provides less energy while too much arousal lets feelings and reactions show, damaging focus and concentration.

One method many professionals use is the "click on, click off" method. A round of golf is long, often 5 hours for 18 holes. Nobody can stay focused the entire time for that long. But since it is crucial to find the optimal level of concentration for each shot, many professionals develop the ability to click on their concentration when they are about to hit the shot. Phrases such as "step into the bubble" describe such preparation for a shot. Inside the bubble, good players will not let anything disturb them. After they play the shot, they step out of the bubble and might chat with the caddie or other players until it is time to step into the bubble for the next shot. The level of clicking on or off varies with the individual player. For example, Lee Trevino once said he could not play if he could not talk to the crowd or the other people around him. He had a very short period of clicking on. Other players, such as Nick Faldo, prefer not to talk during the round; it seems their period of clicking on runs from the first to the last shot of the round. Most likely, though, there is a difference in the level of concentration when playing a shot and when walking to the ball after a shot. Good players have the ability to stay inside the bubble when playing a shot and do not let internal or external distractions disturb them.

PRESHOT ROUTINE

The importance of using a specific preshot routine is under debate. Research has not been able to show that improving the preshot routine improves performance. However, many players and coaches use a consistent preshot routine to help prepare for the shot and shut out internal and external distractions. The preshot routine can be thought of in two ways:

1. The physical routine players go through when preparing for a shot. This involves the number of practice swings, the way the players aim and set up, the time of the routine, and so on.

2. The state players set themselves in before playing a shot. This can be accomplished by a certain routine, but players who are aware of their state and listen to internal signals may not need a specific physical routine, or they may need different physical routines each time to achieve the same state.

Without doubt, the most important part of the preshot routine is the state you are able to put yourself in before you step up to hit the shot. Good players can put themselves in a state of trust and comfort most of the time during a round.

One of the old-time major winners, Arnold Palmer, once had a 15-foot (4.5-meter) putt for a championship. When it was his turn, he just walked up to the ball and played the shot, which he holed. Afterward he was asked about what happened to his routine and why he did not read the putt. He replied, "I already knew how to play the shot and did not want to disturb that by having second thoughts."

FIND YOUR ZONE

Athletes in all sports try to find the zone. The zone is a state in which everything seems easy—an optimal state of performance. For many golfers, that includes picturing the hole as being much bigger than it actually is, seeing fairways as wider than they are, and visualizing a path for the ball to roll into the hole. Players who have experienced the zone also say that while in the zone they do not think about failure and they have a very clear view of what they need to do (seeing the target and not the water hazard, for example).

Misstep

While playing a shot, you are worrying about a water hazard, out-of-bounds area, or bunker instead of concentrating on executing the shot.

Correction

This problem is often the result of not having made a clear decision on what to do for the shot. A clear decision means seeing, hearing, and feeling the shot, which will help keep out distractions. Try the masters drill (page 146) and imagine the pressure or nervousness that might distract you. The think box and play box drill (page 145) also may help.

The zone is probably not a state that others can teach you how to reach. Most likely you have experienced a state like this before, either on or off the golf course. With a few cues, you can experience it again and note some of the characteristics that will help you find it again and again.

The first mental focus drill, My Winning Formula (page 143), will help you identify times when you have experienced the zone. It will also help you identify what the experience was like in terms of what you saw, how you felt, and what you heard. Perhaps your posture and body language are important. For example, you probably won't go around feeling sorry for yourself if you have a smile on your face. Body language can affect the physics in the body. When you know what your zone is like, the cues that describe it, and the things you can do to get there, it will be much easier for you to find the zone by choice rather than chance. The second mental focus drill, Reliving Your Winning Formula (page 144), will help you practice your cues and identify your progress in finding them on the golf course.

THINK BOX AND PLAY BOX

Golf is a game that involves a great deal of thinking. Course strategy, decision making for each shot, club selection, and other aspects must be considered. At the same time, the golf swing is a complex motor task. Conflictive thinking such as doubts about decisions you've made, thoughts about how to swing, or worries about the outcome of the shot increase the chance of bad shots.

One way to deal with this conflict is to separate thinking from playing with a decision line.

Do all your thinking behind the ball in the think box. The thinking involves deciding what type of shot and trajectory to hit, what club to use, and how to swing in order to produce the desired shot. When you have made your decision, cross the decision line, step up to the ball, and play the shot in the play box. Playing the shot is simply executing it. If you sense conflicting thoughts or worries, step back behind the decision line and reconsider your decision.

Misstep

You are unable to reach the level of concentration you need for a shot.

Correction

Thinking about other things can be a problem for any player. Any distracting thought, game-related or not, will take attention away from the shot. Perform the rehearsal drill (page 147) to increase your awareness of the task. Compare the execution with the rehearsal and adjust.

Before hitting the shot, imagine it with as many senses as you can. Visualize the shot as it flies toward the hole, hear the sound of the club smacking the ball, and feel the swing. Not every golfer is able to visualize; for some people, other senses are stronger. You may find it easier to hear the shot or recall how it feels to execute it. Jack Nicklaus once said he always plays a shot twice: first he sees it in his mind and then he actually does it. If that works for you, great; if not, find another way to mentally rehearse your shots.

Plan of Action

1. Develop a basic game plan for the round, including when to be aggressive and when to play it safe.

2. For the shot at hand, decide what you want to do: what type of shot to hit (ball flight and trajectory), what club to hit, and how to execute the shot (setup and swing).

3. Make sure you have a clear idea of where the ball should land (target).

4. Imagine with as many senses you can what the shot will be like (visualize the shot, hear the sound, and feel the swing).

5. Step up to the ball and execute the shot.

6. If anything distracts you—noise, movement, or negative thoughts—step back, clear your thoughts, and go again.

Misstep

You find yourself thinking ahead to a possible score when you are playing well or you dwell over a shot you missed earlier.

Correction

Not staying in the present is a problem for many players. What you need to do right now should have your utmost attention. Try the think box and play box drill (page 145). Whenever your thoughts turn to things that will not help you, raise a "stop" sign and return to where you want to be.

Mental Focus Drill 1. *My Winning Formula*

Sit or lie down in a place where you won't be disturbed. Relax and think back to a time when you experienced the zone—a round on the golf course, a game in another sport, or some other occasion when things went your way. Remember this event as vividly as you can. Try to experience in your mind everything that happened. Ask yourself, "What did I look like? What was my body language like? How did I walk? Was I slow or quick? What did I see? What did I hear? How did I talk to myself? What was my voice like? What did I feel? What did I think?"

While focusing on this event, or right after, make a list of things that you thought or experienced during that zone experience. These factors are probably what helped you reach the zone. Common factors for golfers include the following:

- I am focused on the shot at hand.
- I walk with my head held high.

- All I see is where the ball should land.
- I trust my swing and my instincts.
- I follow my routine and I am relaxed.

Do this exercise 10 times over a period of time such as one or two weeks and rate your success as follows:

- Cannot see, hear, or feel anything; previous experiences are gone = 0 points
- Can visualize an experience close to the zone but it is not golf-related = 1 point
- Can see or hear previous good performances on the golf course = 2 points
- Find something to add to your winning formula = 3 points
- Gain the confidence that you can experience this formula again during play = 4 points

To Decrease Difficulty

- Have somebody videotape you when you are playing. Watch the tape and try to reexperience your thoughts and feelings during play.
- Make notes during a round while you are experiencing the zone.

To Increase Difficulty

- Think about the zone while practicing and try to incorporate it into your shots.
- Discuss your zone experience with a friend and compare notes.

Success Check

- Relax, think back, and let whatever comes up come up.
- Make notes after you finish reliving the experience.

Score Your Success

0 to 5 points = 0 points

6 to 11 points = 1 point

12 to 17 points = 2 points

18 to 24 points = 3 points

25 to 32 points = 4 points

33 points or more = 5 points

Your score ____

Mental Focus Drill 2. *Reliving Your Winning Formula*

When you have identified a number of factors in your winning formula, practice getting to the level you need to reach for each factor that will allow you to play your best. For instance, what does "focused on the shot at hand" mean? Can you be more or less focused, and what will that level do to your performance?

When playing a round, give yourself a grade from 1 to 5 on each factor after you complete each hole. Note your score on each factor. After 3 holes, see what grade has come up most frequently; that is your score for those 3 holes. Every 3 holes, determine your most common score. After 18 holes, calculate your total score by adding the numbers of the six different 3-hole scores.

To Decrease Difficulty

- Start on the putting green and set up 18 holes of putting. Score both the number of shots you take and how well you achieve your winning formula.
- Try your winning formula on the range without the distractions of playing the course.

To Increase Difficulty

- Divide the round into three-hole matches with yourself and score yourself after completing three holes. Try to improve for each three-hole match.
- Ask a partner to distract you when playing shots (see the bubble drill on page 148).

Success Check

- Pay attention to your keys to success.
- Work with your mind-set and body language to come as close as possible to what is best for you.

Score Your Success

Fewer than 7 points = 1 point

7 to 12 points = 2 points

13 to 18 points = 3 points

19 to 24 points = 4 points

25 to 30 points = 5 points

Your score ____

Mental Focus Drill 3. *Think Box and Play Box*

Place a ball on the ground and pick a target for a shot. Place a club as a decision line 4 or 5 feet behind the ball (figure 11.1). The area next to the ball is the play box, and on the other side of the decision line is the think box. Stand in the think box and decide what shot to hit. Pick a club and feel or picture your swing. Cross the decision line and step into the play box. Execute the shot with no thoughts, trusting in your decision. If you are disturbed by anything, step back into the think box and start over. Play 10 balls, scoring yourself based on the following criteria:

- Experience a lot of disturbing thoughts while trying to hit the shot = 0 points
- Make a decision in the think box but lose it when in the play box = 1 point
- Make a decision, try to execute it, but get distracted = 2 points
- Get distracted in the play box and step back to the think box to start over = 3 points
- Make a clear decision and execute it with confidence in the play box = 4 points

To Decrease Difficulty

- Hit with your favorite club until you feel comfortable.

- Try the exercise while putting on the practice green.

To Increase Difficulty

- Hit different types of shots (draw, fade, high, low) and vary your targets.
- Take the exercise to the course and see if you can do it there.

Success Check

- Make sure the decision line is visual so that you can see the think box and play box.
- Any time you can't keep thoughts away in the play box, step back to the think box and start over.

Score Your Success

0 to 5 points = 0 points

6 to 11 points = 1 point

12 to 17 points = 2 points

18 to 24 points = 3 points

25 to 32 points = 4 points

33 points or more = 5 points

Your score ___

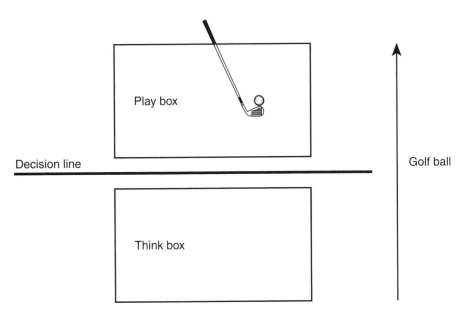

Figure 11.1   Set a club behind the ball as a visual decision line.

Mental Focus Drill 4. *Think Box and Play Box With Partner*

For this drill, do the same thing as in the think box and play box drill but take turns picking a target with a partner. When your partner plays, try to gently disturb him by making noise or moving. If you are distracted by your partner, step back and start over. Play at least five balls each, scoring yourself based on the following criteria:

- Experience a lot of disturbing thoughts while trying to hit a shot = 0 points
- Make a decision in the think box but lose it when in the play box = 1 point
- Make a decision, try to execute it, but get distracted = 2 points
- Get distracted in the play box and step back to the think box to start over = 3 points
- Make a clear decision and execute it with confidence in the play box = 4 points

To Decrease Difficulty

- Hit with your favorite club until you feel comfortable.
- Try the exercise while putting on the practice green.

To Increase Difficulty

- Hit different types of shots (draw, fade, high, low) and vary your targets.
- Take the exercise to the course and see if you can do it there as well.

Success Check

- Make sure you are clear about your decision line so that you can see the think box and play box.
- Any time you can't keep thoughts away in the play box, step back to the think box and start over.

Score Your Success

0 to 5 points = 0 points

6 to 11 points = 1 point

12 to 17 points = 2 points

18 to 24 points = 3 points

25 to 32 points = 4 points

33 points or more = 5 points

Your score ___

Mental Focus Drill 5. *The Masters*

While at the driving range, picture a golf course you know well, such as Augusta National, site of the U.S. Masters, or any course you are familiar with. Start on tee 1 and picture the first hole in front of you. Identify the left and right edge of the fairway, hazards, bunkers, and so on, making the visualization as real as you possibly can. If you have tournament experience or can guess what that might be like, try to imagine the nervousness or pressure you think you would have to deal with. Hit your first shot and determine where the ball would end on your imaginary course. Play your next shot from that position and continue until you reach the green or short-game area. Play at least nine holes. Give yourself 1 point for every fairway you hit off the tee and 2 points for every green you hit in regulation.

To Decrease Difficulty

- Play an easier course with wider fairways and larger green areas.
- Imagine the pins in the middle of the greens.

To Increase Difficulty

- Play a more difficult course with narrower fairways and smaller greens.

- Imagine the pin placements in difficult spots such as behind bunkers or toward the edges.

Success Check

- Go through your normal routine when preparing for each shot.
- Use the decision line, think box, and play box.

Score Your Success

0 to 3 points = 0 points

4 to 7 points = 1 point

8 to 11 points = 2 points

12 to 15 points = 3 points

16 to 19 points = 4 points

20 points or more = 5 points

Your score ___

Mental Focus Drill 6. *Rehearsal Drill*

On the driving range, in the short-game area, or on the course when faced with a particular shot, deliberately go through the preparation for the shot. After deciding which shot to take and how to execute it, rehearse the shot next to the ball, exactly the way you want to play it. Try to store the feeling of the rehearsal shot in your memory, then execute the real shot and compare it to the rehearsal shot. When the rehearsal shot and the real thing match and the shot is good, you are done. If the real shot is not good, think about the differences between the rehearsal shot and the real thing. If there weren't any differences, practice and develop your shot-making skills. If there were some differences, you need practice to be able to perform what you already know so you can play the shot you planned to play. Play at least 10 balls and score yourself based on the following criteria:

- Played the shot but have no clue if it matched the rehearsal swing = 0 points
- Played the shot but it was nothing like the rehearsal swing = 1 point
- Played the shot like the rehearsal swing but it was not a good shot = 2 points
- Played the shot unlike the rehearsal swing but it was a good shot = 3 points
- Played the shot like the rehearsal swing and the shot was super = 4 points

To Decrease Difficulty

- Play five shots with the same club and then another five with a different club.
- Start with short putts and work your way out as you get the hang of it.

To Increase Difficulty

- Make as big a difference between shots as possible. For example, hit a driver followed by a wedge.
- Perform the drill while playing on the course.

Success Check

- Make a clear decision on how you want to execute the shot.
- As vividly as possible, using all your senses, rehearse the shot.
- Play the shot and compare it to your blueprint.

Score Your Success

0 to 5 points = 0 points

6 to 11 points = 1 point

12 to 17 points = 2 points

18 to 24 points = 3 points

25 to 32 points = 4 points

33 points or more = 5 points

Your score ___

Mental Focus Drill 7. *The Bubble*

Golf is often about keeping distractions away. Distractions can come from inside, such as thoughts or feelings that get in the way of playing the shot as well as you can. Distractions can also come from outside, such as noise, movement, or other things that attract your attention. Fortunately, you can prepare to deal with distractions and practice staying in your bubble of concentration.

Team up with a friend and take 10 balls each. For every ball, pick a target, a club, and a shot to hit. When you get ready to play your shot, your partner should try to distract you in different ways, for example, by making a sound, moving, saying something, or simply doing nothing (since you will be expecting something, doing nothing is a distraction). Score yourself based on the following criteria:

- Missed the shot completely = 0 points
- Played the shot but was distracted and did not hit the target = 1 point
- Played the shot, was not distracted, but missed the target = 2 points
- Played the shot, was distracted, but hit the target anyway = 3 points
- Played the shot, was not distracted, and hit the target = 4 points

To Decrease Difficulty

- Play five shots with the same club and then another five with a different club.
- Limit the distractions to a couple of predetermined options.

To Increase Difficulty

- Make as big a difference between shots as possible. For example, hit a driver followed by a wedge.
- Perform the drill while playing on the course.

Success Check

- Make a clear decision on how you want to execute the shot.
- Use the think box and play box.
- Step away and start over if you get distracted.

Score Your Success

0 to 5 points = 0 points

6 to 11 points = 1 point

12 to 17 points = 2 points

18 to 24 points = 3 points

25 to 32 points = 4 points

33 points or more = 5 points

Your score ___

MENTAL AND EMOTIONAL CONTROL SUCCESS SUMMARY

No matter how good a golfer you are, you are not going to hit perfect shots every time. To become a great player, you will need to manage the mental aspects of the game both when playing well and when the game is not so good.

The zone is a state we all know. Finding your way there and staying there is the key to playing at your potential. A number of drills can help you become better at executing shots you actually know how to hit. All of them focus on getting out of your own way since too much thinking usually messes things up. Bob Rotella once said, "People tell me golf is so difficult because the ball is lying still and you have so much time to think.

Then why is it that as soon as it gets important, players take even longer to prepare?"

Record your point totals from each of the drills in this step and add them together. A score of 20 points or more indicates you are on your way to mastering the mental aspects of the game and you're ready for the next step. If you scored 15 to 19 points, you should be able to move on after reviewing and practicing the two drills you find the most difficult. If you scored fewer than 15 points, you have not sufficiently mastered the skills. Practice some more before moving on to the next step.

Mental Focus Drills

1. My Winning Formula	___ out of 5
2. Reliving Your Winning Formula	___ out of 5
3. Think Box and Play Box	___ out of 5
4. Think Box and Play Box With Partner	___ out of 5
5. The Masters	___ out of 5
6. Rehearsal Drill	___ out of 5
7. The Bubble	___ out of 5
Total	___ *out of 35*

You are nearing the end of your journey to golf success. The final step is to develop ways to close in on making par. In the final step, we explore setting goals, practicing with purpose, and moving toward improving on the course.

Closing In on Par

With knowledge of the rules, practiced skills, and an understanding of how to manage your golf game, you are ready to accelerate your journey to become a successful golfer. How good you become will largely be a combination of motivation, practice, playing experience, and increased knowledge. As a game for a lifetime, golf will provide a constant challenge and getting better will never grow old.

The first step to improving your game is understanding your bottom line in playing golf. In other words, at the end of a round what is it that puts a smile on your face and gives you a deep sense of satisfaction? From there you can begin to identify specific goals and establish benchmarks for gauging your success. In this final step, we will discuss goal setting, effective practice, and common benchmarks for measuring success.

SETTING AND REACHING GOALS

Successful performers in any endeavor share one common approach to getting better: They set and achieve realistic, meaningful goals.

Simply swinging a golf club or banging balls time and again does not guarantee improvement in performance. Merely repeating a performance is not practice. To perfect a skill, you must practice with a purpose, or a goal.

Setting practice goals and planning improvement begins with selecting the skills that will make the biggest difference in your performance. Later in this step, we will discuss how

you might go about identifying such skills, but for now it is enough to realize that improvement begins with the setting of a goal. Good practice goals are both meaningful and achievable.

A meaningful practice goal is one that you believe will lead you to increased success. You want to spend most of your practice time working on goals that will lower your scores. For example, you may feel that you cannot stroke the ball with consistent contact to find the fairway, so you set a goal of developing an efficient, repetitive swing.

Full swings account for 35 to 40 percent of the strokes in a round, while the other 60 to 65 percent are partial swings or putts. If you want to make a difference in your game, for every three hours of practice you should devote two hours to the short game. But when you go to most practice facilities, where do you see the majority of golfers? Banging away at the full swing. If that is what you enjoy doing with your practice time, fine. But don't think that your game is going to dramatically improve if you never make it to the short game.

When determining meaningful goals, it is important to have an accurate assessment of your skills prioritized in terms of your success on a golf course. For example, you may not be a particularly good bunker player and still score reasonably well because you don't have to hit that shot very often in a round. However, if your putting is suspect, you should make it a priority because no one finds success in golf without finding success in putting. Becoming a better putter is a meaningful goal for almost every player.

Making your goals achievable means you are able to reach them. Consider two things when identifying achievable goals. First, the goal must be realistic given your ability and physical conditioning. While we would all like to drive a golf ball more than 300 yards, few of us have the ability to do so no matter how much we practice. Second, the goal should be measurable so that you will know when you have reached it. Becoming a better putter is a meaningful goal, but how will you know when you have improved? Setting a standard of comparison is helpful. For example, you may be able to make 5 out of 10 putts from 3 feet. Set a goal of making 8 out of 10 putts and practice for a week or two, then measure whether your goal of becoming a better putter has been achieved.

Pros Need Goals, Too

After a successful career as an international amateur player and collegiate golfer at Oklahoma State University, Anders Hultman turned professional. Some might think that having a résumé that included a national championship while at Oklahoma State would mean that there was little or no room for improvement. That's not the way Anders thinks, though, so he developed a game-improvement plan. He had others review his skills and his playing performance. They were able to identify specific areas that would increase his level of performance. Several goals were set and ranked in terms of which goals would have the largest effect on his performance.

The first goal was fairways hit. Specifically, Anders was hitting 58 percent of the fairways with his tee shots. The very best professionals hit the fairways 70 to 80 percent of the time. Anders set the goal of improving his tee shots so that he finds his golf ball sitting in the fairway more often when he is playing a tournament. With this goal in mind, specific drills were suggested, and Anders now spends a considerable amount of his practice time working on this skill. By the way, the rest of the goals were related to the short game, and they receive a healthy amount of Anders' attention in practice.

Because it is critical to achieve the goals you set, set no more than three goals at a time. Too many goals make it difficult to focus during practice, which makes it difficult to reach your goals. Pick out only the most meaningful goals that will increase your golfing success.

In the next section, we discuss benchmarks of success, or ways to determine how much progress you are making, and then we suggest ways these benchmarks can help you speed up your success.

Misstep

You set goals but never seem to reach them.

Correction

Make sure your goals target specific skills and are measurable. It is difficult to improve with a vague goal such as "I want to shoot lower scores." That kind of goal does not identify a skill that will lead to a lower score. A goal such as "I want to have more one-putt holes" will help you find appropriate practice activities that will lead to achievement.

Goal-Setting Drill. *Priority Goals*

Review the rating of your goal skills that you completed in step 10 (My Most Successful Shots, page 122). Identify the shots you need to improve the most and design two practice goals that specifically state how you will know you have achieved success. For example, you might state, "My goal is to be able to chip 8 out of 10 balls to within 3 feet of a hole that is 10 yards away on a practice green."

Success Check

• Make sure goals are measurable and achievable.

Score Your Success

For each goal, give yourself 1 point if you identify a specific skill and 1 point if you identify the level of success you hope to achieve.

Your score ___

DEVELOPING SKILLS

Few people enjoy doing anything poorly, and golfers seem to be particularly passionate perfectionists. While it is sometimes difficult to see immediate results from practice and learning on the golf course, there are many benchmarks of success that are achievable and rewarding. Many professional and amateur golfers set skill-development goals and then craft effective practice regimes to meet those goals. Professionals in particular use on-course performance information to analyze strengths and weaknesses in their games and then set practice goals based on this information. This is an effective strategy that works for golfers of all levels.

First, keep a record of vital statistics while you play a round of golf (figure 12.1). This is rather easy to do if you simply record a little extra information on your scorecard. Basic performance statistics focus on four areas: fairways hit, greens in regulation, putts, and short-game skills. The first two statistics provide an indication of full-swing mechanics; the last two identify player skill within the crucial area 100 yards from the green—the touch shots. Identifying the strongest and weakest areas in your game will allow you to take the second step: setting goals.

The importance of goal setting has already been explained, but let's apply those principles. If you don't hit the fairway very often, it is difficult to get the ball on the green and give yourself a chance to make a putt for a good score. Missing the fairway means finding your ball in the rough, in the trees, in a hazard, or out of bounds. If your game analysis shows that you hit a low percentage of fairways, then this may be an area where you can construct a practice goal. Once a practice goal is set, you are ready for the third step: practice.

153

	Hole									
	1	2	3	4	5	6	7	8	9	Out
Par	4	4	4	5	4	3	4	4	3	35
Yards to green	360	386	307	451	423	174	316	415	141	2,973
Handicap	11	3	13	5	1	15	9	7	17	
Score	5	5	4	5	6	4	4	4	3	41
Fairway hit		X		X	X		X			4/7
Green hit in regulation			X	X			X		X	4/9
Putts	2	2	2	2	2	2	2	1	2	17
Up and down, sand save	NUD	NUD			NSS	NUD		NUD		1/5

NUD: no up and down; NSS: no sand save

Analysis: Fairways hit: 4/7, 57%   Greens hit in regulation: 4/9, 44%
            Putts: 17 (par = 18, 1 under par)   Up-downs, sand saves: 1/5, 20%

Based on the information from this round of golf, the golfer could most quickly improve his score by increasing his percentage of up-downs and sand saves. He should practice chipping, pitching, bunker shots, and putting—short-game skills.

Figure 12.1   Sample nine-hole scorecard with vital performance statistics.

USING PRACTICE TO IMPROVE PERFORMANCE

Golf practice involves knowledge, commitment, and assessment. In other words, you must know what you are working toward and how you are working toward it, you must be committed to achieving that goal and be willing to put in the necessary time, and you must monitor your progress so that once you achieve that goal, you can set and pursue the next goal.

If a performance goal such as hitting 50 percent of fairways was accompanied by the practice goal of hitting 12 out of 20 practice fairways, you could establish a practice routine and monitor your progress. In this case, it might serve you well to review step 5 to remind yourself of proper mechanics and drills to ingrain the techniques of the full swing. You might also want to review step 9 to make sure you are using the club that will give you the greatest accuracy.

Next, commit to a regular practice time throughout the week. This can be as simple as taking practice swings in your living room to review your mechanics, but even better, plan on spending an hour or two several evenings a week at the practice range, working on drills from the preceding steps in this book. Practice with a goal in mind, because practice without purpose achieves nothing. Perhaps the former touring pro Tony Lema put it best in Criswell Freeman's *The Golfer's Book of Wisdom* (1995): "The most common practice error is to drift aimlessly to the range and start banging balls at random. This isn't practice. This is a waste of time. The worst thing you can do is practice your mistakes" (p. 68).

Finally, have a mechanism in place to monitor your progress. To see if you can hit 12 out of 20 practice fairways, go to the practice range, take 20 golf balls, and see how many you can stroke into a fairway, imagining the fairway on the practice range based on landscape characteristics or target flags at a distance and width that represents your normal driving distance. The more often you practice and the more often you check your progress, the quicker you will reach your goal.

Skill development does not always need to be tightly tied to performance, especially for beginners. Setting and reaching practice goals on the practice putting green (making 10 3-foot putts in a row, for example) will speed your progress toward becoming an accomplished putter. Improving skills such as chipping, pitching, or hitting bunker shots or increasing your knowledge of rules or etiquette will make you more successful and the game more enjoyable.

A frequently asked question is how much practice is needed to become a successful golfer. This question has no absolute answer, but there are several ways to judge how much practice you need. Goal setting is the easiest and most efficient way to gauge how long to practice. If you predetermine the standard of performance you wish to achieve in a given practice session, simply practice until you reach that standard. This was how six-time Masters champion Jack Nicklaus determined the length of his practices. He would set a specific goal, such as hit a target green five consecutive times with a 3-wood, and as soon as he reached the goal, that portion of the practice was over. If his only goal that day was to be more accurate with his 3-wood, it might be a short practice day.

Short, frequent practice sessions are more effective than a few marathon practices. If you have three hours per week for practice, it's better to schedule three one-hour practices than a single three-hour practice. Practicing while tired is not effective, and the briefer period will ensure that you remain fresh during the entire practice. More frequent practices also will help your muscles retain the memory of the skill pattern you are attempting to ingrain. For this reason, frequently using a practice station at home to work on short-game skills, putting, or even a few slow-motion full swings every night will speed your progress much more than spending long hours once or twice a month at a fancy practice range.

If you can't get to a practice facility on a regular basis, it doesn't mean you can't practice. The good news is that the skills that normally need the most practice can be practiced at home. Anyone with a flat floor can practice putting. Jack Adler, former golf coach at the University of Oregon, likes to set up a little putting course in his house. He assigns each hole a par score as he sets up holes that go around doorways, move from the carpet to tile, and even go down stairs. If you have even a small patch of grass near your home, you can set up a chipping and pitching station. It is also possible to practice these skills by chipping from small carpet samples to towels or pillows. Ben Hogan practiced pitching for hours in his hotel room while he traveled from tournament to tournament. It can be both fun and easy to set up a small practice station, and a few hours of practice per week will pay off handsomely on the golf course.

Improving Practice Drill 1. *Public Practice Facilities*

Use the Internet or a telephone book to locate several practice areas that are accessible. Call or visit to see the skills that you can practice there. Place a checkmark next to each practice station available at the facility:

- Driving range for full swing (grass hitting stations) ___
- Driving range for full swing (artificial mat stations) ___
- Short-game area (chipping and pitching green) ___
- Short-game area (sand bunkers) ___
- Putting green ___

Visit one facility and take your clubs with you. Score yourself based on the shots you were able to practice at the facility.

Score Your Success

Hit at least 10 balls at the driving range = 3 points

Hit at least 10 chip shots and 10 pitch shots = 5 points

Hit at least 20 putts = 10 points

Your score ___

Improving Practice Drill 2. *Personal Practice Station*

Select a practice goal for a skill you would like to improve. Design a practice station in your home or office. In a one-week period, conduct at least three 20-minute practice sessions.

To Increase Difficulty

- Devise a practice station where you may practice two or more skills.

Score Your Success

Conduct one 20-minute practice session in a week = 2 points

Conduct three 20-minute practice sessions in a week = 5 points

Conduct five 20-minute practice sessions in a week = 10 points

Your score ___

Improving Practice Drill 3. *Game Improvement Plan*

Identify two skills you would like to improve and set two goals to improve them. You may use the goals established in the priority goals drill (page 153) or you may set new goals. Refer to the drills in the appropriate step in this book and select two drills for each goal, then identify where and when you will practice these goals for a two-week period. Record the goals, drills, and practice schedule in figure 12.2.

To Decrease Difficulty

- Establish only one goal.
- Limit practice time to 10 minutes for each drill.

To Increase Difficulty

- Establish three goals.
- Increase the number of drills per goal to four.
- Increase the number of practice days to four or five.

Goal 1 _____

_____

      Drill 1 _____

      Drill 2 _____

Goal 2 _____

_____

      Drill 1 _____

      Drill 2 _____

Practice location _____

Practice days and times

              Day 1 _____   Time _____

              Day 2 _____   Time _____

              Day 3 _____   Time _____

Figure 12.2 Game improvement plan: goals, drills, and practice schedule.

Score Your Success

Set a goal = 1 point per goal

Identify a drill to go with the goal = 2 points per drill

Identify an accessible practice facility = 5 points

Follow game improvement plan for two weeks = 20 points

Your score ___

FINDING A GOOD INSTRUCTOR

Another factor that can speed your progress is locating a good teacher. In *Harvey Penick's Little Red Book* (1992), Penick writes, "Lessons are not to take the place of practice but to make practice worthwhile." Connecting with a good instructor can help make practice more worthwhile.

A good teacher will help you set goals and will suggest practice activities to help you close in on par. Golf instructors are skilled at pinpointing exactly what will make the biggest difference on the course.

When looking for a teacher to help you improve, be sure to consider experience. Full-time instructors who have been on the lesson tee for at least three years are best. If they have been at it for more than 10 years, you know they are good enough to make a living at it. For playing experience, look for someone who was or still is a competitive golfer.

Credentials are the second key factor. Go with a pro. Your time, money, and game are too precious to place in the hands of an amateur. Look for a teacher who is PGA- or LPGA-certified. These individuals have successfully completed a rigorous educational program. To find a teaching professional in your area, try the Web sites for the PGA (www.pga.com) or LPGA (www.lpga.com).

Find a teacher who fits the way you learn. If you like technical, detailed information regarding your swing, look for a teacher who uses video equipment and stresses body position, angles, and swing speed. If establishing a relationship with the teacher is important to your learning, look for someone who focuses on your personal goals, emphasizes motivation and commitment, and asks lots of questions in an attempt to understand you and your game. If you seek a broader approach to learning that encompasses the rich traditions of the game, rules, etiquette, and established techniques in performance, look for the ambassadors of golf who believe golf is more than just chasing a ball for 18 holes. No single teaching philosophy is right for everyone, so decide what best fits your personality. Ask potential instructors to explain their teaching philosophy. The answers should guide your decision.

Simplicity is an art form. The human brain can process only so much information. A great teacher knows the most important piece of information that will make the biggest difference in performance. Lesser teachers will overwhelm you with information in an attempt to cure every symptom they see because they haven't a clue as to what the disease is. When talking with a potential teacher, look for someone who will listen, set one or two goals at a time, and work progressively toward making you a better golfer.

The final key is you. If you are looking for a good teacher, you must be committed to becoming a good student. Practice what your coach tells you to in the way your coach tells you to. No one has ever improved in any sport simply by listening or reading. You've got to do it and do it properly again and again and again. This is why Vijay Singh is one of the best golfers in the world—he practices the most. When you find a good teacher, capitalize on your teacher's advice by applying it.

MEETING BENCHMARKS OF SUCCESS

Depending on your reasons for playing golf and your personal definition of success in the sport, you can use multiple benchmarks to gauge your success in golf.

Practice

By now, you know there is no better way to find success in golf than by practicing the skills that will make you successful. In Freeman's *The Golfer's Book of Wisdom*, Gary Player notes, "The harder you work, the luckier you get" (page 66). To become successful at golf, you must become successful at practice. For many reasons, golfers sometimes find it difficult to regularly get on a golf course. Time, money, access, and physical limitations are just a few of the reasons. Some players find it easier to get to a practice ground than a golf course. Fortunately for these golfers, and all golfers for that matter, practice can be fun and rewarding and offer a benchmark of your success in golf.

Practice can be used as a benchmark in two ways. First, at a practice ground you can find success measured in skill mastery. When practicing your putting, keep in mind a few games or challenges (see step 1 for suggestions) and see if you can improve your score over the last practice. The more skills you can improve and the more your improve in each skill, the more you will improve your overall skill as a golfer.

Second, for a recreational or amateur player, golf must be fun. If it isn't fun, why do it? On the practice ground, you can find pleasure in hitting a well-struck iron shot, splashing a ball out of a bunker, or sinking a dozen putts from a given distance. At our professional training camps, we spend considerable time discussing practice goals, effective drills, and technical information. Late one afternoon at one of these camps, Niclas Fasth, a Ryder Cup player, walked over to one end of the practice tee and started pitching balls to a green about 30 yards away. This wasn't in the practice plan, but as I watched him stroke shots in high, graceful arcs close to the pin, he turned and asked, "Is it OK to just hit shots because it's fun?" Niclas was concerned that inappropriate practice would detract from the high standard he demands from his golf skills. But what he had really done was remind us that golf should be fun. I told him, "Nothing wrong with it at all, Niclas." Enjoying practice is enjoying golf. If you enjoy practice, that is a benchmark of success.

Play

While practicing, learning, and improving should be enjoyable, most golfers measure their success on the golf course. For some golfers, that simply means getting onto a course for a round. Many who have a passion for the game find they don't have the time, money, support, knowledge, or courage to find their way to a golf course. The goal of almost every amateur golfer we know is to play more. This is not only a legitimate goal, it is an important goal. No matter what your reasons for playing this marvelous game, your goals can only be fully realized on a golf course.

To this end, the number of rounds you play, whether they be 9- or 18-hole rounds, should be an important benchmark for your success. Identify the obstacles that prevent you from playing and work toward overcoming those obstacles. For example, find a course near your home that you can get to quickly. This will save you time. Perhaps you can find a municipal or public course that has low green fees or special rates on certain days. This will save you money. Perhaps when talking with friends or your golf instructor you could mention that you would like to find others of your ability and aspirations to play with. This will help you establish the support group with which to play. However you do it, find a way to get to the course. Playing the game is the best way to enjoy the game.

Establish a Handicap

The USGA has developed a handicap system to make play between golfers of different ability levels an even match. A handicap represents the average number of strokes you play over par on an 18-hole golf course.

To establish a handicap, you must report your score, the date you played, and the rating or slope of the course. This information can be submitted to your local club, mailed to the state headquarters of the USGA, or submitted over the Internet. The USGA averages your 10 best scores from the last 20 rounds played, factoring in course difficulty. For example, if your 10 best scores for the last 20 rounds on difficult golf courses averaged 96, your handicap index might be 22, depending on the difficulty of the course.

Raters are trained by the USGA and sent to new courses to rate each course. The raters consider factors such as hole lengths, green sizes, hazards, and fairway widths. After a thorough analysis, the raters give the course two scores: rating and slope. The higher the numbers are, the more difficult the course. This information is found on the scorecard for the course.

A handicap index serves two purposes. Its original purpose is to allow players of different abilities to play against each other competitively. For example, a player with a handicap of 22 who played against a player with a handicap of 12 would be allowed 10 extra strokes (the difference between the handicaps), one stroke on each of the 10 most difficult holes on the course. The second purpose is to serve as a benchmark of success. If your handicap falls from 22 to 20 in the course of a season, you are improving. Ultimately, improvement is measured in your score on an 18-hole golf course, and your handicap is the best measure of your scoring average.

If you wish to establish a handicap or simply seek more information, you can inquire at any golf course or contact the USGA directly through their Web site at www.usga.org.

Participate in Tournaments

Most people who play golf do so for the sheer joy of playing. Golf offers a wonderful opportunity to apply your skills in a beautiful outdoor environment. Today's golf courses often resemble well-manicured parks and botanical gardens. You can also often find myriad social activities surrounding a golf course or club.

Golf is also a competitive game, and many players wish to take their game beyond the recreational level by testing their skills against other players in a tournament. The pressure found in a tournament tests your skill, knowledge, and fortitude. A tournament is a challenge that many players relish, though tournaments are not for everyone. You can gain a lifetime of enjoyment from golf without ever playing a competitive round.

However, if you believe competitive golf is a benchmark of your success as a golfer, you should try a tournament. For amateurs, the most competitive tournaments are hosted by the USGA, although state golf associations also host highly competitive tournaments. Private organizations and charities host tournaments for players who want a challenge but have limited time to commit to serious practice or extensive travel. Information on local tournaments is generally available at your local golf courses.

The two most common competitive formats are stroke play and match play. In stroke play, the player with the lowest number of strokes in a round is declared the winner. Stroke play is the format most often used on professional and collegiate tours. In match play, players compete to win the hole. The player with the lowest score on a particular hole wins the hole. The player to win the most holes is declared the winner. This format is most commonly seen in the Ryder Cup, Walker Cup, Solheim Cup, and similar team events but can also be used in individual competitions such as the World Match Play Championship.

Two other common formats are four-ball best ball and alternate shot. Four-ball best ball is played in pairs. Each golfer in a foursome plays her own ball. The lowest score recorded by a pair on each hole is the one that is recorded. Alternate shot is also played in pairs, and as the name suggests, one ball is played by the pair, with each member of the pair alternating turns. Player 1 tees off, player 2 plays the second shot, player 1 plays the third shot, and so on. Shots are alternated so the same player does not always tee off. These two formats are also popular in team competitions.

A format often used in amateur events is the scramble. The scramble is normally played in pairs but can also be played in threesomes or foursomes. Each player tees off on every hole. The team decides which drive is best and then each player on the team plays his second shot from that spot (one club-length drop). The team decides which second shot is best and they play from there, continuing until they hole the ball. Scores are recorded as stroke play, so only the shots that were actually used to put the ball into the hole are counted, regardless of which partner hit the shot that was used. This format is popular because it gives the average golfer the chance to record scores like they see the pros shoot.

SUCCESS SUMMARY

Record your point totals from each of the drills in this step and add them together. If you scored at least 40 out of 67 points, you are able to plan effective practice sessions that will allow you to close in on par. If you scored 30 to 39 points, you are almost there. Move on after reviewing the sections you feel you can improve the most.

If you scored fewer than 30 points, review the information and go through the drills again to raise your scores. Understanding how to set goals, tailor drills to meet your goals, and arrange a functional practice schedule at an appropriate facility are keys to your continued success as a golfer.

Goal-Setting Drill

   1. Priority Goals   ___ out of 4

Improving Practice Drills

   1. Public Practice Facilities   ___ out of 18

   2. Personal Practice Station   ___ out of 10

   3. Game Improvement Plan   ___ out of 35

Total   ___ *out of 67*

While this brings us to the end of the book, it hardly brings you to the end of your quest to become a successful golfer. We encourage you to regularly revisit the steps to success to remind yourself of the key points that will make you successful and practice the drills. The techniques for putting, strategies for planning a practice round, and drills for pitching your ball close to the hole are all here. Only with knowledge and practice will you continue the climb to success in golf.

You can measure success in golf in many ways. To find the measures that will give you most satisfaction, begin by understanding why you desire to play this wonderful game. If your motivation is social or recreational, simply enjoy the camaraderie of your companions and the beauty of the golf course. If you are more competitive, develop a goal-based practice schedule and systematically chart your progress as you improve.

Golf has played a major part in our lives, both as players and coaches. We have enjoyed many beautiful places, met some wonderful people, suffered more than a few disappointments, and celebrated some unforgettable successes. No one has yet perfected this game, although players such as Jack Nicklaus, Annika Sörenstam, and Tiger Woods seem to come remarkably close. Like life itself, golf remains a challenge for us all. We can always get better, but we need to remember to rejoice in the rewards that playing golf brings. Golf is a game that can be enjoyed for a lifetime, and it is our hope that this book has helped you on your way to becoming a successful golfer. Now it is time to put this book down. Go play. Enjoy.

◪ About the Authors

Paul Schempp is a professor of Kinesiology at the University of Georgia, where he is the director of the Sport Instruction Research laboratory. He is a scientific consultant for *Golf Magazine*, in which he assists in the selection of America's Top 100 Golf Instructors. He also serves on the National Education Advisory Board for the Ladies' Professional Golf Association (LPGA) and is a performance consultant for the Swedish Golf Federation.

Schempp holds an EdD in human movement studies from Boston University. A resident of Athens, Georgia, he enjoys spending his free time playing golf, fly fishing, and scuba diving.

Peter Mattsson is the head coach of the Swedish national men's and women's golf teams, coaching both amateur and professional players. He has coached Swedish teams and individual Swedish players at numerous European and World Amateur Championships, at the World Cup, and at professional events on the men's and women's tours. Mattsson holds a BEd in physical education and is currently enrolled in doctoral studies at the University of Orebro. Mattsson has also published a number of golf books in Swedish.

STEPS TO SUCCESS SPORTS SERIES

The *Steps to Success Sports Series* is the most extensively researched and carefully developed set of books ever published for teaching and learning sports skills.

Each of the books offers a complete progression of skills, concepts, and strategies that are carefully sequenced to optimize learning for students, teaching for sport-specific instructors, and instructional program design techniques for future teachers.

The *Steps to Success Sports Series* includes:

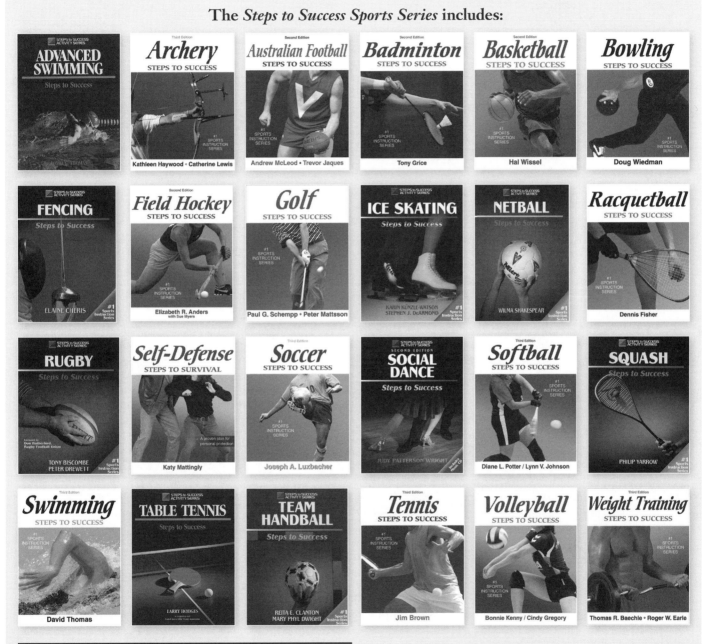

- **ADVANCED SWIMMING** — Steps to Success
- **Archery** — STEPS TO SUCCESS — Third Edition — Kathleen Haywood • Catherine Lewis
- **Australian Football** — STEPS TO SUCCESS — Second Edition — Andrew McLeod • Trevor Jaques
- **Badminton** — STEPS TO SUCCESS — Second Edition — Tony Grice
- **Basketball** — STEPS TO SUCCESS — Second Edition — Hal Wissel
- **Bowling** — STEPS TO SUCCESS — Second Edition — Doug Wiedman
- **FENCING** — Steps to Success — ELAINE CHERIS
- **Field Hockey** — STEPS TO SUCCESS — Second Edition — Elizabeth R. Anders with Sue Myers
- **Golf** — STEPS TO SUCCESS — Paul G. Schempp • Peter Mattsson
- **ICE SKATING** — Steps to Success — KARIN KÜNZLE-WATSON STEPHEN J. DeARMOND
- **NETBALL** — Steps to Success — WILMA SHAKESPEAR
- **Racquetball** — STEPS TO SUCCESS — Dennis Fisher
- **RUGBY** — Steps to Success — TONY BISCOMBE PETER DREWETT
- **Self-Defense** — STEPS TO SURVIVAL — A proven plan for personal protection — Katy Mattingly
- **Soccer** — STEPS TO SUCCESS — Joseph A. Luxbacher
- **SOCIAL DANCE** — Steps to Success — SECOND EDITION — JUDY PATTERSON WRIGHT
- **Softball** — STEPS TO SUCCESS — Third Edition — Diane L. Potter / Lynn V. Johnson
- **SQUASH** — Steps to Success — PHILIP YARROW
- **Swimming** — STEPS TO SUCCESS — Third Edition — David Thomas
- **TABLE TENNIS** — Steps to Success — LARRY HODGES
- **TEAM HANDBALL** — Steps to Success — REITA E. CLANTON MARY PHYL DWIGHT
- **Tennis** — STEPS TO SUCCESS — Third Edition — Jim Brown
- **Volleyball** — STEPS TO SUCCESS — Bonnie Kenny / Cindy Gregory
- **Weight Training** — STEPS TO SUCCESS — Third Edition — Thomas R. Baechle • Roger W. Earle

To place your order, U.S. customers call
TOLL FREE **1-800-747-4457**
In Canada call 1-800-465-7301
In Australia call 08 8372 0999
In Europe call +44 (0) 113 255 5665
In New Zealand call 0064 9 448 1207
or visit **www.HumanKinetics.com/StepstoSuccess**

HUMAN KINETICS
The Premier Publisher for Sports & Fitness
P.O. Box 5076, Champaign, IL 61825-5076